SYSTEMATIC THEOLOGY FOR KIDS

52 Weekly Lessons Exploring Big Questions and Biblical Truth Through a Guided Year-Long Program in Christian Doctrine for Faith-Building

Jasper Trippier

Disclaimer

This book is intended for educational and spiritual purposes only. While every effort has been made to ensure accuracy and faithfulness to Christian teaching, interpretations may vary among denominations and traditions.

The author is not responsible for any personal decisions made by readers based on the content of this book. Readers are encouraged to study Scripture, pray, and seek guidance from trusted spiritual leaders.

This book does not replace pastoral, theological, or professional counsel.

TABLE OF CONTENTS

SYSTEMATIC
THEOLOGY
For KIDS

INTRODUCTION

1. What Is Theology? (Big Word, Simple Meaning)

The word **theology** might sound very big and tricky, but it is actually very simple and very fun. Theology just means **learning about God.** That's it!

When you look at the night sky and wonder, "Who made all those shiny stars?" — you are doing theology.

When you ask, "Does God love me?" — you are doing theology.
When you ask, "Why did Jesus come to earth?" — you are doing theology too!

You don't have to be a grown-up, a teacher, or a pastor. You just need a curious heart that wants to know God better. God loves it when children ask questions!

Learning about God is like learning about your very best friend. The more you learn, the more you understand Him. The more you understand Him, the more you can love Him. God wants us to know Him. He talks to us through the Bible. He shows us His love through Jesus. And He helps us understand with His Spirit.

Theology is for kids, families, and everyone. Children can know that God is good. Children can know that God made the world. Children can know that Jesus loves them. Theology is mostly about love. It teaches us that God is kind, patient, strong, gentle, and always caring for His children. When we learn about God, we also learn how to live. If God is kind, we try to be kind. If God forgives, we try to forgive. If God loves us, we learn to love others too. Knowing God helps us become better friends, better helpers, and better sharers.

Theology also teaches us something very special: **we are not accidents.** God made us on purpose. God knows our names. God loves us deeply.

Jesus shows us what God is like. The Holy Spirit helps us follow God every day. And God is always close to His children, even when we cannot see Him.

So when you hear the word **theology,** don't think of something hard or boring. Think of learning about the One who made you, who loves you, and your forever Friend.

2. Why Learning About God Matters

Learning about God matters because God made us, loves us, and walks with us every day. He knows our names, our thoughts, and our feelings. When we learn about God, we learn that our lives have purpose. We are not here by accident. We are here because God wanted us.

Children learn that God loves them before they do anything good or bad. God's love does not depend on being perfect, behaving well, or being smart. God loves us because we are His. This helps our hearts feel safe, wanted, and never alone.

The Bible teaches that we are made in God's image. This means our lives are precious. We are not perfect, but we are deeply loved. Our words, choices, and actions matter.

Learning about God helps us understand right and wrong in a kind way. God's guidance is not meant to hurt us, but to protect us. It helps us choose kindness instead of cruelty, honesty instead of lies, and forgiveness instead of anger.

When life feels hard, God is still near. He listens when we cry. He understands when we are confused. He stays close when our hearts feel heavy. God does not promise an easy life, but He promises to never leave us.

Jesus shows us what God is like. Jesus was gentle with children, kind to hurting people, and forgiving to those who made mistakes. The cross shows how much God loves us. God's love is stronger than our sins, our fears, and our failures.

Learning about God helps us forgive others and love people better. It teaches us to care for those who are different, to help those who are sad, and to share what we have. Little by little, God shapes our hearts to be more like His.

Learning about God gives us gratitude, hope, and courage. We begin to notice God's gifts around us. We learn to trust God with the future. We learn that failure is not the end, because God always offers new beginnings.

Children are never too small to know God. Jesus loved children and welcomed them. God loves teaching young hearts because they are open and honest.

Prayer becomes a friendship with God. We can talk to Him when we are happy, sad, thankful, or afraid. We also learn that we belong to God's family and to His story.

Learning about God is not about being perfect. It is about growing in love, step by step. It is a journey, not a race. Learning about God brings real joy. Joy means knowing we are safe in God's love. Nothing can separate us from Him.

Learning about God matters because God matters — and you matter to God. He wants you to know Him, love Him, and walk with Him every day.

Learning about God is one of the greatest gifts you will ever receive.

3. How to Use This Book

This book is here to help you learn about God in a simple, gentle, and joyful way. It is divided into 7 units and 52 small sections, so you can learn step by step, little by little, just like walking on a happy path with God.

You do not need to rush. You can read one section each day, one each week, or whenever you feel ready. Learning about God is not a race. It is a journey you walk slowly with Him.

You can use this book by yourself, with your family, or with a teacher. You can read in the morning, in the afternoon, or before bed. There is no wrong way to read this book. The best way is the way that helps your heart feel close to God.

When you read, go slowly. Think about what you read. Ask yourself what you learned about God, about Jesus, and about yourself. If something feels hard, that is okay. You can come back to it later, ask someone for help, or ask God to help you understand.

You may want to write or draw what you learn. You can keep a notebook where you write one sentence, draw a picture, or write a short prayer. This helps your heart remember what you learn.

This book is not meant to replace the Bible. The Bible is God's true Word. This book only helps you understand the Bible better. God speaks most clearly through His Word.

After you read, take a moment to talk to God. You can thank Him, ask Him for help, or tell Him what you learned. Prayer helps your heart stay close to God.

You do not need to understand everything right away. God is patient. He teaches you little by little. What matters is that you keep walking with Him.

This book is not about being perfect. It is about growing. Each section is one small step closer to knowing God better.

Use this book with joy, with peace, and with an open heart. God is happy that you want to know Him.

4. How to Read the Bible

The Bible is God's special book. It is not just an old story. It is God speaking to us with love and truth. When we read the Bible, we are listening to God.

You do not need to be big or very smart to read the Bible. You only need a heart that wants to learn. God is happy when His children open His Word.

Before you read, you can pray simply, "God, please help me understand." God loves to answer that prayer.

Read slowly. Even a few verses are enough. It is better to understand a little than to rush. Let the words stay in your heart.

Ask simple questions: What is happening? What does this show about God? What does this show about people? These questions help you learn.

Sometimes the Bible tells stories. Sometimes it teaches or gives promises[1] . Even when a part feels hard, God is still speaking with love.

If you do not understand something, that is okay. You can ask God or ask a grown-up. God is happy when we ask questions.

It is good to start with Jesus. When we learn about Jesus, we learn what God is like. Jesus helps us understand the whole Bible.

The Bible shows real people who trusted God and people who made mistakes. This reminds us that God loves real people like us.

Try to remember one small truth each day. Maybe God is kind. Maybe God forgives. Maybe God keeps His promises. One truth is enough.

The Bible gives comfort when we are sad, courage when we are afraid, and joy when we are thankful. It helps us pray and trust God.

Sometimes we forget what we read, but God's Word still works in our hearts, like seeds growing quietly.

The Bible tells one big story of God's love. When you read it, remember that God is with you and loves you.

The Bible is God's gift to you — and He gave it because He loves you.

[1] A promise is when God says, "I will take care of you."

5. Our Learning Map

Learning about God is like going on a journey. When you travel, a map helps you know where to go. This book is your learning map. It helps guide you as you discover who God is and how much He loves you.

You do not need to understand everything at once. You only need to take one step at a time. Each lesson is one small step that brings you closer to knowing God better. God walks with you on every step, even when you feel unsure.

First, you will learn about God and His Word. You will learn that God is loving, powerful, and good, and that He speaks to us through the Bible. Then you will learn about creation and people, and how God made us special even when we make mistakes. After that, you will learn about Jesus, who shows us God's heart and saves us.

Next, you will learn about the Holy Spirit, who helps us understand and follow God. You will learn about salvation[2] , which means being forgiven and given new life. You will learn about the church, God's family, and how we belong together. Finally, you will learn about the future, when God will make everything new and full of joy.

This map is not meant to confuse you. It is meant to help you feel safe and hopeful. You do not have to be perfect. You only have to keep walking and learning.

This journey is not just about learning ideas. It is about building a friendship with God. He is not waiting far away at the end. He is walking with you right now.

Your learning map leads to one beautiful truth. God loves you, God wants you, and God is always with you.

And every step you take brings you closer to His heart.

---

[2] Salvation means God says, "I forgive you. I love you. You belong to Me." God makes your heart clean and gives you a happy new start.

UNIT 1 — God and His Word

Welcome to Unit 1! In this first unit, you are going to learn the most important thing of all: who God is and how He speaks to us. Think of this unit like the first steps on a safe, bright path. Before we learn about anything else, we begin with God—because everything starts with Him.

In these pages, you will learn that God is not far away or hard to know. He is real, loving, and close. He made you on purpose, He knows your name, and His love does not change. You will also learn a comforting truth: there is only one true God—not many. That means you never have to wonder who is in charge or who to trust. God is steady, strong, and good.

Then you will learn about something wonderful and mysterious: God is three in one—the Father, the Son (Jesus), and the Holy Spirit. This does not mean three gods. It means one God whose life is full of perfect love and unity. This helps us understand that God's love is not lonely—God's love is alive and always reaching toward us.

You will also learn that God has always been God. He has no beginning and no ending. That means His love is not new or temporary. It is strong forever. And because God is holy and good, His heart is safe. He never does wrong, and He always chooses what is best.

Finally, this unit will teach you how God speaks: through the Bible. The Bible is God's Word—His true, loving message to us. And the Bible has one clear goal: it points us to Jesus, the One who shows us God's heart.

Take your time in Unit 1. Read slowly. Ask questions. Pray simple prayers. Every page is helping your heart learn something steady and beautiful: God is good, God is near, and God loves you.

1. Who Is God?

Look around you. You can see the sky, trees, animals, people, colors, and light. None of this happened by accident. Someone loving and wise made it all. That Someone is God.

God made everything — the stars, the oceans, the birds, and the tiny flowers. He also made you. You are not here by mistake. You are here because you were wanted.

We cannot see God with our eyes, but He is real. We cannot see the wind or love either, but we know they are real. God is living and close to us, even when we cannot see Him.

God is not like people. He never gets tired, confused, or sick. He never forgets or makes mistakes. His understanding is perfect, and His heart is always good.

God is not just a power or an idea. He is a Person who loves, listens, and cares. He knows your thoughts and your feelings. Nothing about you makes Him stop loving you.

God's love never runs out. It never breaks. It never leaves.

Kindness, gentleness, truth, and goodness are part of who He is. His power created the universe, yet His power is loving and safe.

God is holy, which means He is perfectly good and pure. His holiness shows us what real love looks like.

Even though He is bigger than the universe, He is very close. He is near when you laugh, when you cry, when you sleep, and when you wake.

He knows your name. He knows your fears and your joys. He knows when you feel strong and when you feel weak. And He loves you in every moment.

Love is not just something God does. Love is who He is. His love does not stop when you make mistakes. His love stays.

God is patient and gentle. He listens to every prayer. Every tear matters to Him. God speaks through the Bible and through Jesus. His words bring peace, truth, and hope.

He cares about right and wrong. He protects the hurting. He never breaks His promises. His mercy gives people new beginnings.

Nothing surprises Him. Nothing is too broken for His care.

God rules with love, not anger. He leads gently, like a shepherd caring for sheep.

We were made to know God, love Him, and walk with Him. He is not far away. He is near, like a hand that can hold yours.

Jesus shows us what God is like. When Jesus loved, forgave, and helped, God was showing His heart.

Children are precious to God. Questions matter. Small prayers matter. Hurt feelings matter.

God never changes. His love stays strong. His promises stay true.

He is alive and loving right now.

God is our Creator, Father, Protector, Teacher, Savior, and Friend. He holds the universe in His hands, and He also holds your heart.

There is no need to be afraid.

2. There Is Only One True God

Imagine looking up at the night sky and seeing many tiny lights. They look small, but they are huge stars far away. Now imagine someone saying each star has its own god. That would be confusing. Which one would really be in charge? The Bible gives us a simple and comforting answer: **there is only one true God.** One loving, powerful, living God.

This is good news. It means the world is not ruled by many fighting powers. Love is not divided. Truth is not confused. Goodness has one strong source. Everything truly kind, beautiful, and right comes from the same loving heart.

Long ago, people made many gods for the sun, rain, sea, money, and power. They hoped these things would protect them. But those gods were not real. They could not speak, love, or save. The true God is not made by people. People are made by Him.

The true God carries the world. He sees everything. He hears every prayer. Nothing surprises Him. Nothing can stop Him.

Because there is only one true God, we never have to wonder who to trust. His plans are strong. His love is steady. His power is never weak.

This truth is not meant to scare us. It is meant to give us peace. Just like your body has one heart that gives life, the world has one God who gives life to everything.

Because there is only one God, every person matters. No one belongs to a different god. No one is invisible. The same God who made you made everyone else.

Some people think one God must be far away or too busy. But the opposite is true. His love is complete. His care is personal. He gives His full attention.

The Bible teaches that God spoke and created everything. Light came. Land appeared. Life began. This shows that no one is like Him.

Because there is only one true God, our hearts do not need to be divided. Money, fame, strength, or success cannot love us back. Only God can forgive, heal, and save.

The true God protects our hearts. He knows that false things can hurt us. He invites us to trust His love instead.

Our prayers go to the right place. We never have to wonder who is listening. The One true God hears us.

This God is alive right now. He loves right now. He watches over us right now.

He does not change. His love stays strong. His promises stay true. His goodness stays bright.

There is one God who made you.
There is one God who knows you.
There is one God who loves you.

He is not afraid of your questions. He welcomes your learning. He invites you to know Him.

He is near in prayer, gentle in teaching, and strong in love.
He is the beginning of everything.
He is the center of everything.
He is the hope of everything.

There is no other like Him.

Only one true God — and He loves you deeply, completely, and forever.

3. God Is Three in One

Sometimes we hear something that makes us stop and think. When someone says, “God is one, but also three,” it can sound confusing at first. Our minds may ask, “How can that be?” But this truth is not meant to confuse us. It is meant to show us how wonderfully full and loving God is.

There is only one God. Not many. Not a group. One true God. But inside this one God, there are three Persons who live in perfect love and unity. These three are the Father, the Son, and the Holy Spirit. They are not parts of God. Each one is fully God. They are not mixed together, and they are not separated. They are different, yet perfectly united.

This truth is called the Trinity[3]. The word Trinity means three in one. It is a special word we use to talk about God’s beautiful mystery.

Think about the sun. The sun gives light, warmth, and heat. Light is not warmth. Warmth is not heat. But all of them come from the same sun. The sun is still one sun. In a gentle way, this helps us understand how God can be one and yet show Himself in three loving Persons.

Or think about a family. A mother, a father, and a child are three different persons, but they are one family. They share love, life, and belonging. God is even more perfect than any family, but this helps us imagine how love can live inside unity.

The Father is God.
Jesus the Son is God.
The Holy Spirit is God.

They are not three gods. They are one God who lives in perfect love.

Before the world was made, God already existed as Father, Son, and Spirit. This means God was never lonely. Love already existed inside God. Joy already existed inside God. Sharing already existed inside God. Love is not something God learned later. Love is who God has always been.

When God made the world, He was not trying to fill an empty place. He was sharing His love. Creation was an invitation for others to know His joy.

When Jesus came to earth, He showed us what God is like. He loved children. He helped the sick. He forgave sinners. He welcomed the broken. Everything Jesus did showed the heart of God. At the same time, the Father was caring, and the Spirit was working. God was never divided.

When Jesus was baptized, something beautiful happened. Jesus was in the water. The Spirit came down like a dove. The Father spoke from heaven. Three Persons, one God, working together in perfect harmony.

This helps us understand that God's life is full of unity. There is no fighting inside God. There is no jealousy. There is no pride. There is only love, joy, and peace.

The Father plans with love.
The Son saves with love.
The Spirit helps with love.

But they always work together.

When the Father sent Jesus, He did not stop being God. When Jesus lived on earth, He did not stop being God. When the Spirit came to live in believers, He did not stop being God. God was not divided. God was shared.

The Trinity shows us that unity does not mean everyone is the same. It means everyone is perfectly connected in love.

This is why God wants people to love each other. We are made to reflect His own life. When we love, forgive, and care, we are showing a small picture of God's heart.

The Trinity also teaches us that God is close. The Father loves you. Jesus loves you. The Spirit loves you. Not with three different loves, but with one perfect love. Every part of God is for you.

When you pray, you are not talking to a far and lonely God. You are talking to a God whose heart is full. When you feel comforted, the Spirit is helping you. When

---

3 The Trinity means God is Father, Jesus, and Spirit. They are not three gods. They are one God who loves together, works together, and never stops loving you.

you learn about Jesus, you are seeing God's kindness. When you trust the Father, you are resting in God's care.

Some things about God are still mysterious. We cannot understand everything. But mystery does not mean something is wrong. Mystery means something is bigger than us.

A child may not understand how the heart beats, but the heart still beats. A child may not understand how a bird flies, but the bird still flies. In the same way, we may not understand everything about the Trinity, but God is still perfectly true.

The Bible does not try to explain the Trinity with long and hard rules. It shows the Trinity through love, story, and action. It lets us see God working in perfect unity.

Because God is three in one, love is always moving. Love is always giving. Love is always reaching out. The Father reaches to us. Jesus reaches to us. The Spirit reaches into us.

This means we are not just watching God's love. We are invited into it.

When you feel loved, you are touching God's heart.
When you forgive, you are reflecting God's heart.
When you help, you are sharing God's heart.

God is not cold.
God is not distant.
God is living love.

The Trinity shows us that God's love is not quiet or still. It is active. It moves toward people. It rescues, heals, teaches, and comforts.

And this living love has always been reaching toward you.

You are not outside of God's love. You are inside it.

The Father knows you.
Jesus walks with you.
The Spirit lives near you.

One God.
Three Persons.
Perfect love.

This is not a puzzle meant to confuse your heart. It is a truth meant to fill your heart with wonder, peace, and joy.

And the more you grow, the more beautiful this truth will become.

4. God Has Always Been God

Have you ever asked where everything began? Where did the sky come from? Where did the earth come from? Where did people come from? And then a bigger question appears in your mind: where did God come from?

This question is very special, because God is the only One who did not come from anywhere. God has always been God.

Before there was a sun, God was there. Before there was a moon, God was there. Before there was a world, God was there. Before there was time, God was there. Nothing made God. Nothing started God. Nothing taught God how to be God. He has always been alive, always been loving, always been powerful.

Everything else has a beginning. Flowers grow from seeds. Babies grow in their mothers. Houses are built by workers. Even mountains were formed over time. But God was never formed. God never grew into God. God never learned to be God. He simply has always been.

This may feel hard to imagine, because our minds are used to beginnings. We remember our birthdays. We know when school started. We know when a story begins. But God has no birthday. God has no starting page. God has no first moment.

He simply is.

This does not make God strange. It makes Him wonderful.

Because God has always been God, He is never surprised. Nothing is new to Him. Nothing is confusing to Him. Nothing is too big for Him. He does not need to look for answers. He already knows them.

Because God has always been God, He never gets tired of being good. He never forgets how to love. He never changes His mind about caring for people. His heart has always been full of kindness.

Imagine a light that has never turned off. Imagine a love that has never stopped. Imagine a goodness that has never faded. That is what God is like.

Some people think God is old. But God is not old in a tired way. He is eternal in a living way. He is always fresh. Always strong. Always awake. Always alive.

God does not grow weaker with time. God does not lose memory. God does not lose joy. God does not lose love. He is always full of life.

Because God has always been God, He is not learning how to love you. He has always known how to love. Because God has always been God, He is not practicing how to care for you. He has always cared.

You are loved by a love that has no beginning.

This also means God did not decide to be kind one day. He has always been kind. God did not decide to be patient one day. He has always been patient. God did not decide to be good one day. He has always been good.

God has never been cruel.
God has never been selfish.
God has never been careless.

He has always been God.

When the Bible says God is eternal, it means His life has no edges. It has no walls. It has no ending. It flows forever in perfect goodness.

This gives us great comfort. It means God will never disappear. He will never stop loving. He will never stop watching. He will never stop caring.

Friends may leave. People may move. Feelings may change. But God will always remain.

Because God has always been God, His promises are strong. When He promises to love you, that love is backed by forever. When He promises to forgive, that forgiveness is backed by forever. When He promises to stay with you, that promise is backed by forever.

Nothing in the world can break a promise that comes from an eternal God.

Sometimes children worry that God might forget them. But someone who has always existed cannot forget love. Sometimes children worry that God might change His mind about them. But someone who has always been good does not stop being good.

God's love for you is not new. It is ancient and fresh at the same time.

Before you were born, God loved you.
Before you knew His name, He knew yours.
Before you could pray, He was listening.

This also means God understands every time in history. He understands yesterday. He understands today. He understands tomorrow. He is not trapped in one moment like we are. He sees the whole story.

When something feels confusing to you, it is not confusing to Him. When something feels scary to you, it is already held by His care.

Because God has always been God, He never panics. He never rushes. He never loses control. His heart is calm and strong.

This does not mean God is slow. It means God is steady.

It also means God never needed help to exist. He did not need someone to create Him. He did not need someone to protect Him. He did not need someone to teach Him. He has always been complete.

And yet, even though God needs nothing, He chooses to love.
He chooses to care.
He chooses to speak.
He chooses to rescue.
He chooses to walk with people.

Not because He is lonely, but because He is loving.

God has always been God, and He will always be God. There will never be a time when He is not alive. There will never be a time when He is not good. There will never be a time when He is not near.

This is why we can trust Him with our future. The One who has always been alive can hold tomorrow. The One who has always been good can be trusted with our lives.
When we feel small, we remember He is eternal.
When we feel afraid, we remember He is steady.
When we feel unsure, we remember He is unchanging.

God did not begin loving you when you were born. He has always been love. And His love found you right on time.

You are not loved by a temporary God.

You are loved by an eternal God.
A God who has always been God.
A God who will always be God.

And a God who has always loved you.

5. God Is Holy and Good

Have you ever seen something so clean and beautiful that you did not want to touch it because you were afraid to make it dirty? That feeling helps us understand a little of what the Bible means when it says God is holy [4]. Holy means completely pure, perfectly good, and wonderfully different from anything else. God's heart is never messy. His thoughts are never cruel. His ways are always right.

Holiness does not mean God is far away or cold. It means His goodness is brighter than anything we know. It means His love has no shadows. It means nothing bad can live inside His heart. God never lies. God never hurts people for fun. God never chooses what is wrong. Everything He does is clean, kind, and true.

Goodness is part of who God is. He does not try to be good. He is good. Just like fire is hot and water is wet, God is good. When He creates, He creates good things. When He speaks, He speaks good words. When He acts, He acts with goodness.

Think about the best kindness you have ever seen. Maybe someone helped you when you were sad. Maybe someone shared when you had nothing. Maybe someone forgave you when you made a mistake. All those beautiful moments are tiny reflections of God's goodness.

God's holiness means He is perfect in love. God's goodness means He wants what is best for us.

Sometimes children think holiness means God is always serious and never smiling. But holiness also means joy. God enjoys goodness. He enjoys beauty. He enjoys love. He enjoys seeing His children grow and learn.

Holiness does not make God unkind. It makes Him safe.

Because God is holy, He always protects what is right. Because God is good, He always cares for people. He does not ignore pain. He does not forget tears. He

---

4 Holy means God is very, very good, clean, and full of love. Nothing bad lives in His heart.

does not laugh at suffering. His heart moves toward those who are hurting.

God's holiness also shows us something about ourselves. When we see how good He is, we notice that we are not always good. We make wrong choices. We hurt others. We think selfish thoughts. But God does not turn away from us because of this. Instead, His goodness invites us to grow.

His holiness is not meant to push us away. It is meant to pull us closer and make us better.

Imagine a bright light in a dark room. The light does not hate the darkness. It simply shines and makes the room better. In the same way, God's holiness shines into our lives to heal, guide, and clean our hearts.

God is not holy in a scary way. He is holy in a loving way. He wants us to learn goodness from Him. He wants us to become kind, gentle, honest, and patient.

When Jesus came, He showed us what God's holiness looks like. Jesus did not shout at children. He welcomed them. Jesus did not hate sinners. He helped them. Jesus did not enjoy power. He served others. That is holiness in action.

Goodness also means God always chooses love. Even when people choose wrong, God chooses mercy. Even when people fail, God offers forgiveness. Even when people run away, God invites them back.

God's holiness and goodness work together. Holiness keeps God pure. Goodness keeps God gentle.

Because God is holy, He never stops being right. Because God is good, He never stops being kind.

This is why we can trust Him. We never have to wonder if God will suddenly become cruel. We never have to worry that God will enjoy our pain. We never have to fear that God will forget love.

God's heart is safe.
When we feel ashamed, holiness reminds us that God can clean us.
When we feel broken, goodness reminds us that God can heal us.
When we feel lost, holiness and goodness together show us the right way home.

God does not ask us to be perfect before He loves us. He loves us so we can grow. His goodness teaches us. His holiness protects us. He is not proud. He is

not mean. He is not unfair. He is perfectly right and perfectly kind at the same time.

Imagine a king who is always fair and always gentle. Imagine a judge who always tells the truth and always shows mercy. Imagine a parent who always loves and always teaches what is right. That is what God is like, only greater.

God's holiness means He never does wrong.
God's goodness means He always does what is best.

You never need to be afraid of God's heart. His holiness does not push you away.
His goodness invites you in.
He wants you to learn from Him.
He wants you to trust Him.
He wants you to walk with Him.

When you see something truly good in the world, remember where it came from. When you feel kindness, remember its source. When you see beauty, remember its Creator.

6. God Is Love

Imagine standing outside at night and looking up at the sky. You see many tiny lights shining above you. They look small, but they are actually huge stars far away. Now imagine someone telling you that each star has its own god. That would feel confusing. Which one would you trust? Which one would really be in charge?

The Bible gives us a clear and comforting answer: **there is only one true God.** One loving, powerful, living God.

This is good news. It means the world is not controlled by many fighting powers. It means love is not divided. Truth is not confused. Goodness has one strong source. Everything truly kind, beautiful, and right comes from the same loving heart.

Long ago, people made many gods. Some made gods for the sun, the rain, the sea, money, or power. They hoped these things would protect them. But those gods were not real. They could not speak. They could not love. They could not save. The true God is different. He is not made by people. **People are made by Him.**

The true God does not need help to carry the world. He carries it. He does not need help to see. He sees everything. He does not need help to hear. He hears every prayer. Nothing surprises Him. Nothing is too hard for Him.

Because there is only one true God, we never have to wonder who to trust. We never have to choose between gods. His plans are steady. His love is strong. His power is always enough.

This truth is not meant to scare us. It is meant to give us peace. Just like your body has one heart that gives life, the world has one God who gives life to everything.

Because there is only one God, every person matters. No one belongs to a different god. No one is invisible. The same God who made you made every other person too.

Some people think one God must be far away or too busy. But the opposite is true. His love is complete. His care is personal. He gives His full attention to each child.

The Bible teaches that God spoke and created everything. Light came. Life began. This shows us that no one is like Him.

Because there is only one true God, our hearts do not need to be divided. Money, fame, strength, or success cannot love us back. Only God can forgive, heal, and save.

Our prayers go to the right place. We never have to wonder who is listening. The One true God hears us.

This God is alive right now. He loves right now. He watches over us right now.

He does not change. His love stays strong. His promises stay true. His goodness stays bright.

There is one God who made you.
There is one God who knows you.
There is one God who loves you.

He welcomes your questions. He invites you to learn. He wants you to know Him.

He is near in prayer, gentle in teaching, and strong in love.

He is the beginning of everything.
He is the center of everything.
He is the hope of everything.

There is no other like Him.

Only one true God — and He loves you deeply, completely, and forever.

7. God Speaks to Us

Have you ever wanted to hear someone's voice because you missed them? Maybe a parent, a friend, or someone you love. Hearing their voice makes your heart feel warm and safe. In the same way, God wants us to hear His voice too. And the wonderful truth is this: God is not silent. God speaks.

God does not speak because He is bored. He speaks because He loves. He wants us to know Him. He wants us to understand His heart. He wants us to feel close to Him. A loving God is a speaking God.

Long ago, God spoke and the world began. He spoke light into darkness. He spoke life into nothing. His voice is powerful, but it is also gentle. It can create stars, and it can comfort a child.

God speaks in many ways. He speaks through the Bible. He speaks through Jesus. He speaks through His Spirit in our hearts. He speaks through truth, kindness, and love.

Sometimes children think God only speaks to grown-ups. But that is not true. God loves to speak to children. He listens when children pray. He smiles when children ask questions. He answers in ways that help hearts understand.

God's voice is not loud like thunder most of the time. It is often soft like a whisper. It guides instead of pushes. It invites instead of forces. It comforts instead of scares.
When you feel a gentle thought that says, "Be kind," God may be speaking.
When you feel a quiet reminder to forgive, God may be speaking.
When you feel peace after prayer, God may be speaking.

God's voice never tells us to hate.
God's voice never tells us to hurt.
God's voice never tells us to lie.

His voice always leads us toward love, truth, and goodness.

God also speaks through stories in the Bible. When you read about Noah, Abraham, Moses, David, and Jesus, you are hearing God's voice telling you about His care, His power, and His love.

God speaks through Jesus in a special way. Jesus did not only talk about God. Jesus showed us God. When Jesus spoke, God was speaking. When Jesus loved, God was loving. When Jesus forgave, God was forgiving.

Listening to God is not about using our ears only. It is also about using our hearts. Sometimes God speaks by helping us understand something. Sometimes He speaks by giving us courage. Sometimes He speaks by reminding us that we are not alone.

You may not hear God like you hear a human voice. But you will feel His guidance, His peace, and His love.

God never shouts to scare His children. He leads with patience. He teaches with kindness. He corrects with care.

When we make mistakes, God does not scream. He invites us back.
When we are afraid, God does not push. He comforts.
When we are confused, God does not leave. He guides.

God's voice always matches His love.

Sometimes we are too busy to listen. Sometimes our hearts are loud with worries or excitement. But God is patient. He waits for us to become quiet inside. When we slow down, we begin to notice His gentle voice.

Listening to God is like listening to a caring friend. You do not need to be perfect. You only need to be open.

God also speaks to help us grow. He teaches us what is right. He helps us understand what is good. He reminds us who we are.

When God speaks, He is never trying to make us feel small. He is trying to help us become strong.

When God speaks, He is never trying to confuse us. He is trying to guide us.

When God speaks, He is never trying to hurt us. He is trying to protect us.

God's voice brings life.
And the most beautiful part is this: God wants to speak to you. Not only to pastors. Not only to teachers. Not only to adults. To you.

Your questions matter to Him.
Your thoughts matter to Him.
Your prayers matter to Him.

God speaks because He loves.
God speaks because He cares.
God speaks because He wants to walk with you.

And when you learn to listen, you begin to discover that God has been speaking to your heart all along.

8. The Bible Is God's Word

Imagine receiving a letter from someone who loves you very much. You would want to read it carefully. You would want to know what it says. You would want to keep it close. The Bible is like that letter. It is God's Word for us.

The Bible is not just a normal book. It is not only made of paper and ink. It is full of God's thoughts, God's promises, and God's love. When we read the Bible, we are reading what God wants us to know.

Many people helped write the Bible, but God helped them know what to write. God guided their minds and hearts. That is why the Bible is called God's Word. It comes from Him, even though people wrote it down.

The Bible tells us stories. It tells us about brave people, scared people, kind people, and people who made mistakes. It tells us about kings, children, families, and friends. But in every story, God is teaching us something important.

The Bible teaches us who God is.
The Bible teaches us how God loves.
The Bible teaches us how God helps.

The Bible also teaches us about ourselves. It shows us that we need love, forgiveness, and hope.

Some stories in the Bible are happy. Some are sad. Some are exciting. Some are quiet. But all of them help us learn about God's heart.

The Bible is not a magic book, but it is a powerful book. It can comfort us when we are sad. It can guide us when we are confused. It can remind us when we forget. It can make our hearts brave when we feel small.

The Bible is not only for grown-ups. It is for children too. God wanted children to know His words. That is why the Bible has stories that children can understand.

When you hear a Bible story, God is speaking to your heart. When you read a verse, God is teaching you something true. When you remember a promise, God is giving you hope.

The Bible also helps us know what is right and wrong. It does not shout at us. It gently shows us the better way. It teaches us to love, forgive, share, and be kind.

The Bible is honest. It does not pretend people are perfect. It shows mistakes and forgiveness. It shows fear and courage. It shows problems and hope. This helps us see that God works with real people, just like us.

The Bible also tells us that God keeps His promises. When God says something, He does it. His promises are strong and sure.

The Bible is like a lamp in the dark. It helps us see where to walk. It helps us not to get lost. It helps us feel safe.

When you read the Bible, you are never reading alone. God is with you. He sees you. He listens to your thoughts. He loves that you want to know Him.

You do not have to understand everything in the Bible. You only need to keep listening. God teaches little by little.

The Bible is God's gift to you. He gave it so you would know Him. He gave it so you would know His love. He gave it so you would never feel alone.

Every page is a reminder that God cares.

And every word is a small light showing you His heart.

9. Why We Can Trust the Bible

Imagine you have a friend who always tells the truth. When they promise to come, they come. When they say they will help, they help. After a while, you begin to trust that friend. You know their words are safe. The Bible is like that friend. It is a book we can trust because its words come from a God who never lies.

We can trust the Bible because God is honest. God never tricks people. God never forgets what He says. When God makes a promise, He keeps it. The Bible is full of God's promises, and that is why its words are strong.

Think about a parent who promises to pick you up from school. When they arrive every time, you learn to trust them. In the same way, when God's promises in the Bible come true again and again, we learn we can trust Him.

The Bible was written by many people long ago, but God helped them know what to write. It is like when a teacher tells a child what to write on a paper so the message is correct. God guided the writers so the message would be true and loving.

We can trust the Bible because it tells the truth about people. It does not pretend that people are perfect. It tells us about brave people and scared people. It tells us about people who obeyed God and people who made mistakes. This helps us know the Bible is honest.

For example, the Bible tells us that King David loved God, but it also tells us that he made wrong choices. The Bible does not hide his mistakes. It shows how God forgave him. Honest stories help us trust the book.

We can trust the Bible because it teaches good things. It teaches us to love others, forgive, tell the truth, and help people. A book that teaches kindness and goodness is a book that comes from a good God.

The Bible also helps us when we feel sad or scared. It tells us that God is with us. It tells us that we are not alone. A book that brings comfort to hurting hearts is a book we can trust.

We can trust the Bible because its message stays the same. Even though the Bible has many books inside it, they all tell one big story. God loves people. People make mistakes. God forgives. God saves. God stays with His children.
This story never changes.

We can trust the Bible because God kept His promises in it. God promised to send Jesus, and Jesus came. God promised to forgive, and He does. God promised to stay with His people, and He still does. When promises come true, trust grows.

The Bible is like a flashlight in the dark. When it is dark, you cannot see where to walk. But when you turn on a light, you feel safer. The Bible helps us see what is right and good. It helps us not get lost.

Sometimes the Bible has big words or stories that feel hard. That does not mean we cannot trust it. It only means we are still learning. A child may not understand everything in a math book, but the book is still true. In the same way, we grow in understanding the Bible little by little.

The Bible is not trying to confuse us. It is trying to help us.

You can trust the Bible like you trust a map. Even if you do not know every road, the map still shows the right direction. The Bible shows us the way to God.

You can trust the Bible like you trust a story from someone who loves you. God gave us His Word because He wanted us to know Him.

When you read the Bible, you are not just reading words. You are listening to a loving voice that wants to guide you.

The Bible has helped children, parents, teachers, and families for many years. It has helped people learn to love, forgive, and hope. A book that helps so many hearts is a book worth trusting.

You do not have to understand everything in the Bible to trust it. You only need to know that God is good and His words are true.

The Bible is safe.
The Bible is honest.
The Bible is loving.
And because it comes from God, we can trust it with our hearts.

Now, the Bible has one more beautiful secret.

Every story, every promise, and every lesson in it is pointing us to Someone very special.

And that is what we will learn next.

10. The Bible Points Us to Jesus

Imagine reading a big storybook where every chapter slowly helps you meet the main hero. At first, you only hear little hints. Later, you see clearer pictures. And in the end, you finally meet the hero face to face. The Bible is like that. From the first page to the last page, it is leading us to Jesus.

Some people think the Bible is just a book about rules or old stories. But it is really a book about a Savior. Every story, promise, and lesson is like an arrow pointing in one direction. That direction is Jesus.

In the beginning of the Bible, God makes a beautiful world. But people choose to disobey. Things break. Hearts get hurt. Fear enters. Right away, God promises that He will send someone to fix what is broken. That promise is about Jesus, even though His name is not spoken yet.

Later, the Bible tells stories about people who tried to follow God. Some were brave. Some were kind. Some were scared. Some failed. None of them were perfect. These stories teach us something important. People need help. People need saving. People need a Savior.

That Savior is Jesus.

The Bible tells us about lambs that were offered to God. It tells us about kings who were meant to protect people. It tells us about prophets who spoke God's words. All of these things are like pictures that prepare us to understand Jesus better. Jesus is the true Lamb. Jesus is the true King. Jesus is the true Messenger of God.

When we reach the stories about Jesus, everything becomes clear. Jesus is gentle with children. Jesus is kind to the sick. Jesus forgives those who are sorry. Jesus loves people others ignore. Jesus shows us exactly what God is like.

If you want to know what God's smile looks like, look at Jesus helping someone.
If you want to know what God's mercy looks like, look at Jesus forgiving.
If you want to know what God's love looks like, look at Jesus on the cross.

The cross is not just a sad story. It is a love story. Jesus chose to suffer so we could be forgiven. That shows us that we are very valuable to God. The Bible points to this moment again and again because it is the heart of God's love.

After Jesus rose from the dead, the Bible shows us that love is stronger than death. Hope is stronger than fear. Life is stronger than loss. Jesus is alive, and that changes everything.

The Bible does not end with sadness. It ends with joy. It ends with Jesus promising to come again and make everything new. That tells us the story is not over yet.

Sometimes when you read the Bible, you may see rules. Those rules teach us how to live with love. Sometimes you may see history. That history shows how God keeps His promises. Sometimes you may see songs or prayers. Those show how people talk to God. But all of it is leading to Jesus.

Jesus is the center of the Bible.

Without Jesus, the Bible would be a story about people trying and failing. With Jesus, the Bible becomes a story about God rescuing and loving.

When you read about courage, Jesus is the greatest courage.
When you read about kindness, Jesus is the greatest kindness.
When you read about forgiveness, Jesus is the greatest forgiveness.

The Bible does not only tell us about Jesus. It invites us to know Him.

You do not have to be perfect to come to Jesus.
You do not have to be strong to come to Jesus.
You do not have to be brave to come to Jesus.

You only have to be willing.

Jesus is the reason the Bible exists. He is the reason the stories matter. He is the reason the promises shine.

The Bible is like a road. Jesus is where the road leads.
The Bible is like a light. Jesus is what the light shows.
The Bible is like a gift box. Jesus is the gift inside.

When you open the Bible, you are not just opening a book. You are opening a path that leads to a loving Savior who knows your name, understands your heart, and invites you to walk with Him.

And every time you read, the Bible gently whispers the same beautiful truth:

Jesus is here.
Jesus loves you.
Jesus is for you.

UNIT 2 — Creation and People

Welcome to Unit 2! In this unit, you will learn where everything began and why your life is so important to God. You will discover that the world is not an accident. It was created with love, care, and joy by a wise and gentle Creator. Every sky, every ocean, every animal, and every tiny flower exists because God wanted it to exist.

In these pages, you will learn that God did not only make the world beautiful — He made people special. He gave us hearts to feel, minds to think, and voices to speak. He made us so we could know Him, love Him, and enjoy the world with Him. This means your life has purpose. You were wanted. You were planned.

You will also learn that people are made in God's image. That means every person has great value. No one is small. No one is invisible. No one is without worth. When you love, forgive, create, and care, you are showing a little picture of God's heart.

But Unit 2 also tells a sad part of the story. You will learn about the first wrong choice, and how sin brought pain, fear, and brokenness into God's good world. You will see how sin hurt hearts, friendships, and even the world itself. This helps us understand why life can feel hard sometimes.

Yet this unit is not only about brokenness. It is also about hope. You will learn that God did not turn away from His hurting world. He did not stop loving His people. Instead, He made a promise to rescue. He promised that love would not lose, and that healing would come.

As you read Unit 2, remember this:
God made the world.
God made you.
And God's love is already working to make broken things new.

Take your time. Read slowly. Let your heart see how deeply you are loved by your Creator.

11. God Made Everything

Close your eyes and imagine a time when there was nothing you could see. No sky. No trees. No animals. No people. No colors. No sounds. Just quiet. And then… God smiled and decided to create[5].

God did not need tools. He did not need help. He did not need a long time. He simply spoke, and wonderful things began to appear.

First came light. Bright, warm, happy light. Darkness moved away, and the world began to glow. Then God made the sky high above and the land below. He made oceans that sparkle and rivers that dance. He made hills, valleys, and tall mountains that touch the clouds.

God looked at what He made and said, “This is good.”

Then He filled the world with life. He made trees that wave in the wind. He made flowers with soft petals and bright colors. He made fruit that tastes sweet and leaves that whisper when they move.

God made animals next. He made fish to splash in the water and birds to fly in the air. He made animals that run fast and animals that move slow. He made animals that roar and animals that chirp. He even made tiny bugs that crawl and help the world work.

Each animal was different. Each one was special. And God loved them all.

God looked again and said, “This is good.”

Then God made the sun to shine in the day and the moon to glow at night. He made stars to sparkle like tiny lights in the sky. He made rain to water the plants and wind to cool the earth.

---

[5] Create means God made something new with love, like drawing a beautiful picture

The world was full of color, sound, and joy.

But God was not finished yet.

He had one more beautiful idea.

God wanted to make someone who could talk, laugh, think, love, and enjoy the world with Him.

So God made people.

Before you were born, God already planned you. He knew your eyes, your smile, and your laugh. He wanted you to be part of His world.

The world was not made by accident. A house does not build itself. A toy does not make itself. A picture does not draw itself. In the same way, the world did not make itself. God made it with love and care.

God did not rush when He created. He enjoyed every part. He made the world to be beautiful, safe, and full of peace.

At the beginning, nothing was broken.
Nothing was hurting.
Nothing was afraid.

Everything worked together like a happy family.

God made mornings and evenings. He made seasons. He made time so the world could grow and change in good ways.

Every sunrise is like God saying, “Here is a new gift.”
Every sunset is like God saying, “Rest now.”

God made the world so we could enjoy it. He made colors so we could see beauty. He made sounds so we could hear music and laughter. He made food so we could taste goodness. He made touch so we could feel hugs.

Even the smallest things remind us of God’s care. A tiny flower shows His gentleness. A big mountain shows His strength. A soft cloud shows His creativity.

Sometimes we forget to notice these things. But when we stop and look, we can see God’s love everywhere.

When you see the sky, remember God made it.
When you see animals, remember God made them.
When you look at yourself, remember God made you.

God did not make the world to be boring. He made it to be wonderful.

God did not make the world to be scary. He made it to be good.

God did not make the world and then leave it. He still cares for it every day.

You are living inside God's beautiful creation. You are walking on God's design. You are breathing in God's gift.

And the best part is this: God made all of it because He loves.

The world is not just a place to live. It is a gift from a loving Creator.

And that Creator is God.

12. God Made People Special

After God made the sky, the land, the oceans, and the animals, the world was already beautiful. It had colors, sounds, and life. But God was not finished. He wanted to make someone who could enjoy the world, care for it, and love Him back. So God made people.

God did not make people the same way He made trees or stars. He made people with special care. He gave them hearts to feel, minds to think, and voices to speak. He gave them hands to help and feet to walk. God looked at people and was very pleased, because they were different from everything else He had made.

People were made to love and to be loved. They were made to laugh, to learn, to wonder, and to grow. They were made to enjoy the world and to enjoy God. This is why people are special.

Animals are wonderful, but they cannot pray. Trees are beautiful, but they cannot talk to God. Stars are bright, but they cannot choose to love. Only people can do these things. Only people can know God in their hearts.

Every person is special, not just some. Babies are special. Children are special. Grown-ups are special. Old people are special. Tall people, short people, loud people, quiet people, strong people, and gentle people are all special to God. No one is extra. No one is forgotten.

When God made you, He did not rush. He did not copy someone else. He made you on purpose. Your smile, your voice, your way of thinking, and your way of feeling were all part of His loving plan. You are not a mistake. You are a gift.

People are special because God loves them deeply. He watches them. He listens to them. He cares about their joys and their tears. When someone is happy, God is glad with them. When someone is sad, God stays close to them.

God also made people to take care of the world. He trusted people with animals, plants, and land. He wanted people to protect what He made, not hurt it. He wanted people to help each other and live in peace.

People were made for joy. God loves to see children play, families hug, and friends laugh together. He enjoys kindness. He enjoys sharing. He enjoys love.

People were also made to belong. No one was meant to be alone. God made families, friendships, and communities so people could care for each other. When someone feels lonely, God wants others to show love. When someone is hurting, God wants others to help.

Sometimes children think they are too small to matter. But God never thinks that. Jesus welcomed children. He listened to them. He loved them. He said children are very important in God's kingdom. That means your voice matters to God. Your heart matters to God.

People are special because they can choose. They can choose kindness. They can choose forgiveness. They can choose love. These choices make the world brighter.

Even when people make wrong choices, God does not stop loving them. He does not throw them away. He wants to help them grow and begin again. His love is stronger than mistakes.

When you look at other people, you can remember that God made them too. When you see someone different from you, you can remember they are special. When you see someone sad, you can remember they are precious to God.

And when you look at yourself, you can remember the same truth.

You were made by God.
You are loved by God.
You are special to God.

Not because of what you can do, but because you are His.

13. We Are Made in God's Image

Have you ever looked in a mirror and seen your face staring back at you? You might notice your eyes, your smile, or your hair. But the Bible says something even more amazing. It says that when you look at yourself, you are also seeing a little picture of God. That is what it means to be made in God's image.

Being made in God's image does not mean we look like God on the outside. God does not have a body like ours. It means we are like Him on the inside in special ways. God gave us hearts that can love, minds that can think, and spirits that can know Him. These gifts make people different from everything else God made.

Animals are wonderful, but they do not wonder about God. Trees are beautiful, but they do not choose kindness. Stars are bright, but they do not forgive. People can do these things because they are made in God's image.

Being made in God's image means you can love. You can care when someone is sad. You can share when someone has less. You can forgive when someone hurts you. Every time you love, you are showing a little picture of God's heart.

It also means you can think. You can learn new things. You can ask questions. You can imagine. You can create drawings, stories, songs, and games. God is a Creator, and He made you creative too.

Being made in God's image means you can choose. You can choose to be kind or unkind. You can choose to tell the truth or a lie. You can choose to help or ignore. These choices are important because they show what is in your heart.

Being made in God's image also means you can talk to God. You can pray. You can thank Him. You can ask Him for help. You can tell Him when you are happy or sad. God made you so you could know Him and walk with Him.

Every person in the world is made in God's image. Not just strong people. Not just smart people. Not just healthy people. Babies are made in God's image. Children are made in God's image. Old people are made in God's image. People who feel broken are still made in God's image.

This means every person has great value. No one is useless. No one is trash. No one is too small. No one is too broken. God's image is still there.

Sometimes people forget this and treat others badly. But God never forgets. He always sees His image in every person. That is why He cares so much about people. That is why He wants us to care too.

When you see someone different from you, remember they are made in God's image. When you see someone hurting, remember they are made in God's image. When you see someone who made a mistake, remember they are still made in God's image.

And when you feel sad about yourself, remember this truth too.

You are made in God's image.

You are not just a body.
You are not just a name.
You are not just a number.

You are a person created to reflect God's love.

Being made in God's image does not mean we are perfect like God. We still make mistakes. We still get angry. We still get selfish sometimes. But God's image in us means we can grow. We can learn. We can change. We can become more loving.

God wants His image in us to shine. He wants our kindness to shine. He wants our honesty to shine. He wants our forgiveness to shine. He wants our love to shine.

When we help others, God's image shines.
When we forgive, God's image shines.
When we care, God's image shines.

Jesus showed us the perfect picture of God's image. When we look at Jesus, we see what God's heart looks like in a person. Jesus loved, healed, forgave, and welcomed everyone. He showed us how God wants His image to shine in us.

God made you in His image because He wanted you to be close to Him. He wanted you to reflect His goodness. He wanted you to belong to His family.

You are not here by accident.
You are not here without purpose.
You are not here without value.

You are made in God's image.

And that means your life is precious, your heart is important, and your story matters to God.

14. The First Wrong Choice

At the beginning, God made the world beautiful and peaceful. People were happy. They were not afraid. They walked with God and trusted Him. Everything worked the way it should. God gave people many good gifts and only one simple rule to protect them. That rule was not meant to hurt them. It was meant to keep them safe.

But one day, something sad happened. People were given a choice. They could trust God, or they could choose their own way. Instead of listening to God, they chose to disobey. This was the first wrong choice.

The first wrong choice was not just about eating or touching something. It was about trust. God had said, "This is not good for you." But people believed another voice instead of God's voice. They thought they knew better than God. And when they made that choice, something inside their hearts changed.

Before that moment, people felt close to God. After that moment, they felt ashamed. They wanted to hide. They felt fear for the first time. The world did not look the same anymore.

The wrong choice did not mean God stopped loving people. But it did mean that sadness, pain, and brokenness entered the world. Trust was hurt. Peace was broken. Love was wounded.

This first wrong choice is what we call sin. Sin means choosing our own way instead of God's way. It means not trusting God's goodness. It means turning away from His love.

Sin is not just about big bad actions. Sometimes it is about small choices, like lying, being mean, refusing to share, or ignoring someone who needs help. All of these choices come from the same broken place in the heart.

After the first wrong choice, people realized something important. They could not fix their hearts by themselves. They needed help. They needed God's love to heal what was broken.

God did not yell at them. He did not leave them. He did not stop caring. Instead, He came close. He spoke to them. He still loved them, even though they had made a wrong choice.

This shows us something very important about God. He hates sin, but He loves people. He does not stop loving when we fail. He wants to help us come back.

The first wrong choice did not end God's story. It began a rescue story.

From that moment on, God began working to heal the world. He promised that one day He would fix what was broken. He promised that love would win.

When we make wrong choices today, we sometimes feel the same things. We feel sad. We feel ashamed. We want to hide. But God is still the same. He still wants to help. He still wants to forgive. He still wants to bring us back.

The first wrong choice teaches us that we need God. We cannot live without His love. We cannot heal our hearts by ourselves. But it also teaches us that God never gives up on us.

Even when people chose wrong, God chose love.

Even when trust was broken, God planned healing.

Even when the world became hurt, God began His rescue.

This is why the first wrong choice is a sad story, but not a hopeless one. It reminds us that we all make mistakes, but we are never alone. God is always ready to forgive, to guide, and to love us back into His arms.

The story of the first wrong choice is not the end. It is the beginning of God's promise to rescue His world.

15. How Sin Hurt God's World

After the first wrong choice, the world did not feel the same anymore. Before, everything was peaceful and safe. People trusted God. They trusted each other. Animals were calm. The earth felt like a happy home. But when sin[6] entered, it was like a crack in something beautiful. The crack started small, but it slowly spread.

Sin is like a sickness in the heart. When a heart is sick, it cannot love the same way. It cannot trust the same way. It cannot choose the same way. Because of sin, people began to feel anger, jealousy, fear, and pride. They started hurting each other with words and actions. They started thinking more about themselves and less about others.

Sin did not only hurt people. It hurt the whole world. Work became hard. Pain entered life. Tears became real. Even the earth felt the change. Plants did not always grow easily. Animals became afraid. Storms and disasters appeared. The world was no longer as gentle as it was at the beginning.

Sin is like breaking a toy. At first, the toy looks fine. But when you try to use it, it does not work the way it should. In the same way, sin broke the way people were meant to live with God and with each other. Hearts that were made for love began to struggle with hate. Hands that were made to help sometimes began to hurt.

Because of sin, people started to blame each other. They started to hide. They started to feel lonely even when they were together. Families fought. Friends argued. Nations went to war. All of this pain began with that first broken trust.

But sin did not only hurt relationships. It also hurt hearts. People began to feel fear. They worried about tomorrow. They felt unsure about their worth. They forgot how deeply God loved them. Sin made people feel far from God, even though God was still near.

Sin also made people forget who they were. They were made in God's image, but they began to act in ways that did not look like God's love. Instead of kindness, there was cruelty. Instead of honesty, there were lies. Instead of forgiveness, there was anger.

The world became a place where good and bad lived together. You could see beauty and brokenness at the same time. You could see love and pain in the same family. You could see laughter and tears in the same day.

Even today, we still see how sin hurts God's world. We see people hurting others. We see unfairness. We see sickness. We see sadness. We see loss. All of these things remind us that the world is not the way God first made it.

But here is the most important truth. Sin hurt the world, but it did not stop God's love.

---

[6] Sin means making a wrong choice that hurts love. It makes hearts sad, but God still loves us and wants to help us.

God did not look at the broken world and walk away. He did not give up. He did not forget His children. Instead, He looked at the brokenness with a loving heart and began to plan healing.

God still loved people.
God still loved the world.
God still wanted to rescue what was hurt.

Sin made the world sick, but God prepared the medicine.
Even when people chose wrong, God chose to stay. Even when hearts were broken, God prepared to heal them. Even when the world became messy, God began His rescue story.

This is why we do not lose hope when we see pain. We remember that God is greater than sin. We remember that love is stronger than brokenness. We remember that God is still working.

Sin hurt God's world, but it did not win.

God's love was already moving.

And God's rescue was already on the way.

16. God's Promise to Rescue Us

After sin hurt God's world, life was no longer the same. People still tried to love, but they also made mistakes. They still wanted to do good, but they often chose wrong. The world felt broken in many places, and hearts felt heavy. But God did not stop loving His creation. He did not turn away. He did not give up. Instead, He made a beautiful promise.

God promised to rescue.

This promise meant that the broken world would not stay broken forever. It meant that sadness would not win. It meant that mistakes would not be the end of the story. God was saying, in a gentle and loving way, "I will help you. I will fix what is broken. I will bring you back to Me."

God knew that people could not fix their hearts by themselves. He knew they needed help, just like a child needs help when they fall and scrape a knee. And just like a loving parent runs to help, God ran toward His people with love.

God's promise was not about punishment. It was about healing. It was not about anger. It was about kindness. He wanted people to feel safe with Him again. He wanted them to trust Him again. He wanted them to know they were still His children.

God began telling people about this promise. He told families, leaders, and children. He reminded them that He had not forgotten them. Even when people made more wrong choices, God stayed faithful. Even when people felt far from Him, God stayed close. This promise gave people hope. When they felt sad, they remembered that God was still working. When they felt ashamed, they remembered that God still loved them. When they felt lost, they remembered that God had a plan.

God's promise was not rushed. He was patient. He waited for the right time. And when the time was right, He kept His promise in the most beautiful way.

He sent Jesus. Jesus was God's rescue with a face. Jesus was God's love walking among people. When Jesus helped the sick, God was rescuing. When Jesus forgave sinners, God was rescuing. When Jesus loved children, God was rescuing. And when Jesus gave His life, God was rescuing the world.

God did not rescue by hurting people. He rescued by loving them. He did not rescue by pushing people away. He rescued by coming close. He did not rescue by shouting. He rescued by giving His heart.

God's promise to rescue us means that no one is too broken for His love. It means no one is too small to matter. It means no mistake is too big for forgiveness. God's promise tells us that love is stronger than sin.

Even today, the world is still healing. There are still sad things and hard days. But God's rescue is still working. His love is still changing hearts. His kindness is still bringing hope.

UNIT 3 — Jesus Our Savior

Welcome to Unit 3! In this unit, you will meet the center of the whole Bible story: Jesus. If Unit 1 showed you who God is, and Unit 2 showed you the world God made (and how it became broken), Unit 3 shows you God's rescue with a face and a name. Jesus is God coming close—close enough to be held, close enough to be heard, close enough to be trusted.

In these pages, you will learn that Jesus is not only a teacher with kind words. He is God's Son, and He is also God Himself. That means God did not stay far away in heaven and watch people suffer. He stepped into our world with love. Jesus became fully human—He felt hunger, tiredness, sadness, joy, and pain—so He could truly understand us. And at the same time, He stayed fully God—strong enough to forgive, heal, and save.

You will also see what Jesus is like. He is gentle with children. He notices the lonely. He helps the sick. He welcomes people who feel messy or ashamed. He shows us what God's heart looks like in real life. When Jesus loves, God is loving. When Jesus forgives, God is forgiving. When Jesus comforts, God is comforting.

Unit 3 will help you understand why Jesus came. He did not come to show off power or to become famous. He came because hearts were broken and God wanted to heal them. Jesus came to bring people back to God—to clean what sin made dirty, to lift what pain pushed down, and to give new life and new hope.

This unit also walks through the biggest parts of Jesus' story: how He lived, what He taught, why He died, and why it matters that He is alive. His death was not the end. It was love carrying what we could not carry. And His resurrection means love is stronger than death, forgiveness is real, and hope is not a dream.

And finally, Unit 3 points your heart forward: Jesus promised He will come again and make everything right. That means the story is moving toward a beautiful ending—one full of peace, joy, and home.

As you read Unit 3, go slowly. Let your heart see Jesus clearly. Because Jesus is not only someone to learn about. He is someone who loves you, listens to you, and invites you to walk with Him—one gentle step at a time.

17. Who Is Jesus?

Imagine meeting someone who is kinder than anyone you know, braver than any hero in a story, and gentler than the softest hug. Imagine someone who knows your name, understands your feelings, and loves you even when you make mistakes. That person is Jesus.

Jesus is not just a character from an old book. He was a real person who lived on earth. He walked on dusty roads, talked with people, ate with friends, and helped those who were hurting. He laughed, cried, and cared deeply. And even though He lived long ago, He is still alive today.

Jesus is God's Son, but He is also God Himself. This means God did not stay far away in heaven. He came close to us. He chose to be born as a baby so we could understand Him better. He wanted to show us what God is really like. When we look at Jesus, we are seeing God's heart.

Jesus grew up just like other children. He learned to walk, talk, and work. He knew what it felt like to be tired and hungry. He knew what it felt like to be happy and sad. Because of this, Jesus understands us. He knows what it is like to be human.

But Jesus was also different. He never chose to do wrong. He never lied. He never hurt others on purpose. His heart was always full of love. Everything He did came from kindness and truth.

People loved being near Jesus. Children felt safe with Him. Sick people trusted Him. Lonely people felt noticed. Even people who had made big mistakes felt hope when they met Him. Jesus did not push anyone away. He welcomed them.

Jesus did not act like a proud king. He did not try to look important. He listened. He helped. He cared. He washed people's feet. He shared food. He spoke gently. He showed that true greatness is loving others.

When people asked who He really was, Jesus showed them with His life. When He healed, He showed God's kindness. When He forgave, He showed God's mercy. When He loved, He showed God's heart. Jesus did not only talk about love. He lived it every day.

Jesus also told people that He came to save them. To save means to help hearts come back to God. It means to fix what is broken inside. It means to give new life and new hope. Jesus came because God did not want anyone to stay lost or afraid. That is why Jesus is called our Savior. He came to help us when we could not help ourselves.

Jesus is also our Friend. He listens when we pray. He understands when we feel sad. He cares when we feel afraid. He celebrates when we are happy. He never gets tired of us.

We do not need to be perfect to come to Jesus. We do not need to be brave or smart or strong. We only need to come with open hearts. Jesus never turns away someone who wants to know Him.

Jesus is gentle, but He is also strong. He faced pain without running away. He faced hate with love. He faced death with courage. And He did not lose. His love was stronger than everything.

Jesus is not only part of history. He is part of our lives today. He is alive. He is near. He is still loving, helping, and guiding people.

When we talk to Jesus, He hears us. When we think about Him, He sees us. When we trust Him, He walks with us. He is not far away. He is close to every heart that calls His name.

Jesus is God coming close to people. Jesus is love with hands and feet. Jesus is hope that never ends.

And the more we learn about Jesus, the more we discover that He is not just someone to know about. He is someone to love, trust, and follow.

18. Jesus Is God and Man

Have you ever tried to imagine someone who is both very big and very small at the same time? Someone who is strong enough to make the world, and gentle enough to hold a baby? That may sound impossible, but that is exactly who Jesus is. Jesus is fully God and fully human.

This means Jesus is not half God and half man. He is completely God and completely human at the same time. He did not stop being God when He became a human. And He did not pretend to be human. He truly lived as one of us.

When Jesus was born, He did not come as a king with a crown. He came as a baby in a simple place. He needed to be fed. He needed to be held. He needed to grow. This shows us that Jesus understands what it feels like to be small and weak.

Jesus learned to walk just like you did. He learned to talk. He learned to work. He felt hungry. He felt tired. He felt happy. He felt sad. He knew what it was like to be a child and to grow up. This is the part where Jesus is truly human.

But at the same time, Jesus did things only God can do. He healed sick people. He calmed storms. He forgave sins. He knew what was in people's hearts. He loved perfectly. He spoke with authority. He showed power over death. This is the part where Jesus is truly God.

Jesus did not use His power to show off. He used it to help. He did not use His greatness to make others feel small. He used it to lift people up. This is why people felt safe with Him.

Because Jesus is human, He understands us. When you feel tired, He understands. When you feel hurt, He understands. When you feel lonely, He understands. He knows what it feels like to live in a body and heart like yours.

Because Jesus is God, He can help us. He can forgive us. He can change hearts. He can give new life. He can bring us close to God.

If Jesus were only human, He could not save the world.
If Jesus were only God, we might not understand Him.

But because He is both, He is the perfect Savior.

Jesus is like a bridge between God and people. One side of Him reaches God. The other side of Him reaches us. And through Him, we can come close to God again. Jesus shows us that God is not far away. God understands our lives. God understands our tears. God understands our joy. God understands our pain.

When Jesus cried, God was showing He cares.
When Jesus laughed, God was showing His joy.
When Jesus forgave, God was showing His mercy.

Jesus is God with a human face.

Jesus is also human with God's heart.

This makes Jesus very special. No one else in history is like Him. No teacher, no king, no hero, no prophet is both God and man. Only Jesus.

Because Jesus is God, we can trust Him.
Because Jesus is human, we can relate to Him.

He is close enough to understand us and strong enough to save us.

When Jesus prays, we learn how to pray. When Jesus loves, we learn how to love. When Jesus obeys, we learn how to obey. His life is our example.

Sometimes children wonder how Jesus can be both God and man. We may not understand everything about it, but we can understand the love behind it. God loved us so much that He chose to come close instead of staying far away.

Jesus did not come as a stranger. He came as a family.

Jesus did not come as a ruler who pushes. He came as a friend who walks with us.

Jesus did not come to show power only. He came to show love.

When we look at Jesus, we are seeing God's heart and a human life together in one beautiful person.

Jesus is God who came near.

Jesus is man who shows us the way.

And because He is both, we can trust Him with our whole hearts.

19. Why Jesus Came

Have you ever wondered why Jesus left heaven and came to earth? Why would someone so powerful choose to be born as a baby? Why would someone so perfect step into a broken world full of pain, sickness, and mistakes? That big question has a beautiful answer.

Jesus came because God loves people.

Jesus did not come to start a new religion. He did not come to become famous. He did not come to show off His power. He came to bring people back to God. He came because hearts were broken, and God wanted to heal them.

From the very beginning, God knew people would need help. He knew they would make wrong choices. He knew they would feel lost, afraid, and ashamed. Instead of giving up on them, God made a plan. That plan was Jesus.

Jesus came to show us what God is really like. Some people thought God was only angry or far away. Jesus showed that God is gentle, kind, patient, and full of mercy[7]. When Jesus hugged children, God was showing His love. When Jesus helped the sick, God was showing His care. When Jesus forgave, God was showing His heart.

Jesus also came to fix what was broken inside us. We were made to walk with God, but sin made us feel far away. Jesus came to bring us back. He came to clean hearts, heal guilt, and give people a fresh start.

Think about a child who gets lost in a big store. The child feels scared and alone. But when the parent finds the child and holds them, everything feels safe again. That is what Jesus came to do. He came to find us and bring us back to God's arms.

Jesus also came to teach us how to live. He showed us how to love others, forgive enemies, care for the poor, and trust God. He did not only tell people what to do.

He showed them with His life.
He showed that love is stronger than anger.
He showed that kindness is stronger than pride.
He showed that forgiveness is stronger than hate

[7] Mercy means being kind and forgiving, even when someone makes a mistake.

Jesus came to show us a better way to live.
But Jesus came for an even bigger reason.

He came to save us.

Save does not only mean from danger. It means from sin, from fear, from shame, and from being separated from God. Jesus came to carry what we could not carry and fix what we could not fix.

Jesus knew His life would not be easy. He knew people would misunderstand Him. He knew some would reject Him. He knew He would suffer. But He still came. He still chose love.

Jesus came because no one was too small to matter.
Jesus came because no one was too broken to be loved.
Jesus came because no one was too lost to be found.

Jesus came for children.
Jesus came for families.
Jesus came for sinners.
Jesus came for the hurting.
Jesus came for the lonely.

Jesus came for you.

Some people think Jesus came only to teach good lessons. But He came to do more than teach. He came to change hearts. He came to bring life where there was death. He came to bring light where there was darkness.

Jesus came so we could know God not as a distant ruler, but as a loving Father.

Jesus came so we could stop being afraid of God and start trusting Him.

Jesus came so we could have hope that never ends.
And here is the most amazing part. Jesus did not come because we were already good. He came because we needed Him. He did not wait for us to fix ourselves. He came to help us be healed.

Jesus came because love moved Him, mercy sent Him, and because God could not stop loving His children.

When you ask, “Why did Jesus come?” the answer is not complicated.

He came to love.
He came to save.
He came to bring us home.

And when you begin to understand that, your heart starts to realize something wonderful.

Jesus did not only come to change the world.

He came to change you with His love.

20. How Jesus Lived

If you could follow Jesus for one day, you might expect Him to live in a big palace with guards and gold. But Jesus chose a very different life. He lived simply, kindly, and close to people. And that is what makes His life so amazing.

Jesus did not wake up every day thinking about Himself. He woke up thinking about others. He looked for people who were sad, sick, lonely, or forgotten. And when He found them, He did not walk away. He stopped. He listened. He cared.

Jesus talked with children like they were important. He did not say, "Go away." He said, "Come to Me." He listened to their questions. He welcomed their smiles. He made them feel safe. Children loved being near Him because His heart was gentle.

Jesus also spent time with people others ignored. He talked with poor people. He ate with people who had made mistakes. He touched people who were sick. He never said, "You are too dirty for me." He said, "You are loved."

Jesus did not live to be famous. He lived to be faithful. He did not try to look powerful. He chose to serve. He washed feet. He shared food. He helped without asking for thanks.

Jesus showed us that real greatness is not about being above others. It is about lifting others up.

When someone was angry, Jesus answered with calm.
When someone was rude, Jesus answered with kindness.
When someone was afraid, Jesus answered with peace.

His life was like a quiet light in a dark world.

Jesus prayed often. He talked with God like a loving Son talks with a Father. He prayed in happy times and in hard times. He showed us that we never have to face life alone.

Jesus also obeyed God, even when it was hard. He trusted God's plan. He trusted God's love. He trusted God's wisdom. His life was a picture of perfect trust.

Jesus told stories to help people understand. He used seeds, sheep, bread, and water to teach about God's love. He did not make things confusing. He made them simple and clear so everyone could learn.

Jesus laughed with friends. He cried with those who were sad. He felt tired. He felt joy. He felt pain. He lived a real human life, and He lived it with perfect love.

People followed Jesus not because He was loud, but because He was loving. Not because He was scary, but because He was safe. Not because He forced them, but because His life was beautiful.

And here is what makes His life so special.

Jesus lived the life we were meant to live.
He loved perfectly.
He trusted completely.
He obeyed fully.
He cared deeply.

He showed us what a heart close to God looks like.
Jesus did not just tell people how to live. He showed them. His life was a lesson of love in action.

When you read about how Jesus lived, you are not just learning history. You are seeing a picture of how God wants our hearts to grow.

And when you realize how Jesus lived, you start to wonder something even bigger.

If Jesus lived like this for us…

What did He teach us?

That is the next beautiful part of His story.

21. What Jesus Taught

When Jesus talked, people wanted to listen. Not because His voice was loud, but because His words felt warm, kind, and true. He did not teach like someone trying to sound smart. He taught like someone who wanted hearts to understand.

Jesus did not begin His lessons with big, hard words. He began with stories. He talked about seeds growing in the dirt. He talked about sheep getting lost. He talked about coins, lamps, bread, water, and families. He used things people saw every day so even children could understand God's love.

One of the first things Jesus taught was that God loves everyone. Not only good people. Not only strong people. Not only smart people. God loves children, poor people, sick people, lonely people, and people who make mistakes. Jesus wanted everyone to know that God's love is for all.

Jesus also taught that love is more important than rules. Rules are helpful, but love is the heart. He taught that loving God and loving others is what matters most. He said that kindness, forgiveness, and mercy make God happy.

Jesus taught people to forgive. He knew forgiveness is hard. But He showed that forgiveness sets hearts free. When we forgive, we let go of heavy anger. Jesus wanted people to live with light hearts, not heavy ones.

Jesus taught people to be kind even to those who are unkind. He taught people to help even when it is not easy. He taught people to share, to care, and to notice those who feel small or forgotten.

Jesus also taught that God listens when we pray. He taught people how to talk to God simply and honestly. He showed that prayer is not about fancy words. It is about real hearts talking to a loving Father.

Jesus taught that we do not need to worry all the time. He pointed to birds and flowers and said God takes care of them. Then He said God cares even more about people. He wanted hearts to feel safe instead of afraid.

Jesus taught that true treasure is not money or toys or power. True treasure is love, kindness, and a heart close to God. He wanted people to want the right things, not just shiny things.

Jesus also taught that everyone can change. No one is stuck being bad forever. No one is too broken to be made new. Jesus believed in new beginnings. He believed in second chances. He believed in hearts being healed.

Sometimes Jesus' words surprised people. He said the greatest people are those who serve others. He said the smallest people matter the most. He said children are important in God's kingdom. He said humble hearts are beautiful.

22. Why Jesus Died

When children first hear that Jesus died, they often feel confused. If Jesus was kind, loving, and good, why would anyone hurt Him? Why would He have to die at all? The answer is not about anger or punishment. The answer is about love.

Jesus did not die because He was weak. He did not die because He lost. He chose to die because He wanted to save us.

Jesus knew that something inside the world was broken. Hearts were broken. Love was broken. Trust was broken. People kept hurting each other and turning away from God. And Jesus knew that this brokenness could not be fixed by rules, promises, or trying harder. It needed love strong enough to heal it.

So Jesus chose to take that brokenness on Himself.

When Jesus went to the cross, He was not thinking about Himself. He was thinking about people. He was thinking about children, families, sinners, and everyone who felt far from God. He was saying, in His heart, "I will carry this so they do not have to."

The cross was not a place of hate. It was a place of sacrifice. Sacrifice means giving something because you love someone else more.

Jesus gave His life so we could be forgiven. Not because God wanted to hurt Him, but because God wanted to save us. The cross shows us how serious sin is, but even more, it shows us how strong God's love is.

When Jesus was hurt, He did not fight back.
When Jesus was mocked, He did not insult.
When Jesus was suffering, He still loved.

That kind of love is powerful.

Jesus died so we could stop being afraid of God. He died so we could come close without shame. He died so we could know that God would rather suffer than lose His children.

Think of a parent who runs into danger to save their child. The parent is not thinking about pain. They are thinking about love. That is what Jesus did for us.

Jesus' death also means that no mistake is too big to forgive. No heart is too broken to heal. No person is too lost to be found. His love reached deeper than our worst wrongs.

When Jesus died, it looked like the end. But it was not the end. It was the beginning of something new.

His death opened the door to forgiveness.
His death opened the door to hope.
His death opened the door to life with God again.

Jesus died because He loved us more than His own comfort. He died because He wanted us to live close to God. He died because love was stronger than fear.

And when we understand why Jesus died, we begin to realize something amazing.

He did not stay dead.

And that changes everything.

23. Jesus Is Alive

After Jesus died, His friends felt very sad and very confused. They thought the story was over. They thought love had lost. They thought they would never hear His voice again. They placed His body in a tomb, which was like a small cave, and closed it with a big stone. Everything felt quiet and dark.

But God was not finished.

Early one morning, some of Jesus' friends went to the tomb. They expected to find the stone and the body. But when they arrived, the stone was moved, and the tomb was empty. Jesus was not there.

At first, they were scared. Then they were surprised. Then they were full of wonder. Jesus was alive.

He came and talked with them. He walked with them. He ate with them. He smiled at them. He showed them His hands. They touched Him and knew it was really Him. This was not a dream. This was not a story. Jesus was truly alive.

Think about a butterfly. First it looks like a quiet little bug. Then it goes into a cocoon. It looks like nothing is happening. But one day, it comes out alive and beautiful. In a much greater way, Jesus came back to life after everyone thought He was gone.

Jesus did not rise because people helped Him. He rose because God's power is stronger than death. Death could not hold Him. The tomb could not keep Him. Love was stronger.

When Jesus came back to life, His friends were no longer afraid. Their tears turned into smiles. Their sadness turned into hope. They knew that everything Jesus said was true.

Jesus being alive means something very important for us. It means that God keeps His promises. It means that love never ends. It means that even when things look finished, God can make something new.

Because Jesus is alive, He can still hear us today.
Because Jesus is alive, He can still love us today.
Because Jesus is alive, He can still help us today.

Jesus is not just a memory. He is living now.

When you pray, Jesus listens. When you feel afraid, Jesus cares. When you feel happy, Jesus is glad with you. When you feel alone, Jesus is near you.

Jesus' friends told everyone they met that He was alive. They were not scared anymore. They were brave and joyful. They knew that nothing was stronger than God's love.

Jesus being alive also means that one day God will make everything new. Just like Jesus rose, God promises new life for His children too. This gives us hope when we feel sad and courage when we feel afraid.

Jesus did not come back to life to scare people. He came back to life to give hope.

He came back to show that love wins.
He came back to show that forgiveness is real.
He came back to show that God is stronger than anything.

Jesus is alive.

And because He is alive, our hearts can be full of joy, courage, and peace, knowing that we are loved forever.

24. Jesus Will Come Again

After Jesus rose from the dead, He spent time with His friends. He helped them believe. He helped them stop being afraid. He reminded them that they were loved. Then one day, Jesus told them something very special. He said He would go back to heaven, but He also said He would come again.

This promise is full of hope.

Jesus did not say, “Goodbye forever.” He said, “I will come back.”

Right now, the world is not perfect. People still get hurt. People still feel sad. People still get sick. People still make wrong choices. But Jesus promised that one day He will return and make everything right.

Think about a room that is messy and broken. Toys are everywhere. Things are cracked. Nothing feels peaceful. Now imagine someone saying, “I am coming back to clean it, fix it, and make it beautiful again.” That is what Jesus promised about the world.

When Jesus comes again, there will be no more tears. There will be no more fear. There will be no more pain. People will not hurt each other anymore. Everyone will feel safe, loved, and joyful.

Jesus will not come again as a baby in a manger. He will come as a loving King. But He will still be gentle. He will still be kind. He will still be full of love.

Jesus will come again to gather His people. That means everyone who loves Him will be with Him forever. No one will be lonely. No one will be forgotten. Everyone will belong.

Some children wonder, “When will Jesus come back?” The Bible does not tell us the day or the hour. But it tells us something better. It tells us that Jesus’ return will be good, loving, and full of joy.

Jesus wants us to live with hope, not fear. While we wait, Jesus wants us to love others, forgive, help, and trust God. He wants our hearts to grow gentle and kind. He wants us to live like His children.
Jesus coming again means the story is not finished yet. It means the ending will be beautiful.

When you feel sad, you can remember Jesus will make things right.
When you feel scared, you can remember Jesus is in control.
When you feel small, you can remember Jesus is coming for His people.

Jesus will come again not to scare the world, but to heal it.

He will come again not to push people away, but to welcome them home.

UNIT 4 — God's Spirit With Us

Welcome to Unit 4! In this unit, you will learn one of the sweetest truths in the Christian faith: God does not leave His children alone. After Jesus finished His rescue and returned to heaven, God did not step back. He came even closer. He sent the Holy Spirit—God's own presence with us, helping us every day.

In these pages, you will meet the Holy Spirit as more than a "feeling" or a "power." The Holy Spirit is a real Person who loves, speaks, guides, and cares. He is fully God—just like the Father and Jesus—and He has always been part of God's beautiful life. That means when you feel helped, comforted, or gently guided toward what is good, God is near you in a personal way.

Unit 4 will show you what the Holy Spirit does in our lives. He helps us understand God and His Word when it feels confusing. He is like a gentle teacher who does not rush, does not shame us, and does not give up. He helps us see Jesus clearly and trust God's love even when we feel unsure.

You will also learn that the Holy Spirit works deeper than our thoughts—He works in our hearts. He helps change us from the inside, little by little, like a seed growing into a strong tree. When we choose honesty, kindness, forgiveness, or courage, the Spirit is helping us grow.

This unit also explains the fruit of the Spirit—the good things God grows inside us, like love, joy, peace, patience, and self-control. These are not just rules to try harder at. They are signs that God is working gently within us. And you will learn about the Spirit's gifts—special ways God helps each person serve others, so His family can love better together.

As you read Unit 4, remember this: you do not have to become good all by yourself. You do not have to figure everything out alone. God is with you. He teaches you, comforts you, strengthens you, and keeps helping you take the next step.

The Holy Spirit is God's kindness walking beside you—every day.

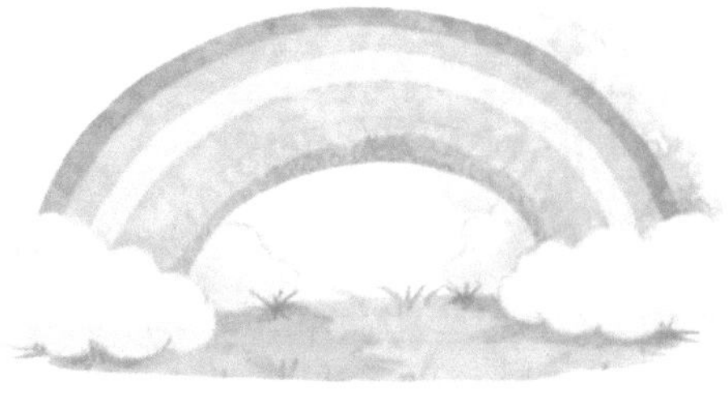

25. Who Is the Holy Spirit?

The Holy Spirit[8] is God with us. He is not just a power, a feeling, or a light. He is a real Person. He thinks, loves, speaks, and cares. The Holy Spirit is fully God, just like God the Father and Jesus the Son.

God is one, but He shows Himself in three wonderful ways: the Father, the Son, and the Holy Spirit. They are never fighting. They are always loving, working together in perfect kindness and truth.

The Holy Spirit has always existed. He was there when God made the world. He was there when the oceans were formed, when animals were created, and when people were made. He was there when Jesus was born, when Jesus taught, when Jesus died, and when Jesus rose again.

When Jesus went back to heaven, He promised He would not leave His followers alone. He promised to send the Holy Spirit. That promise came true. And it is still true today.

The Holy Spirit is God living with His people.

We cannot see Him with our eyes, but we can know Him with our hearts. Just like we cannot see air but we need it to live, we cannot see the Spirit but we need Him to grow.

The Holy Spirit is gentle. He does not push or scare. He guides quietly. He teaches softly. He comforts kindly.

He is strong, but His strength is loving. He is powerful, but His power is peaceful.

He is close when you feel happy.
He is close when you feel sad.
He is close when you feel afraid.
He is close when you feel thankful.

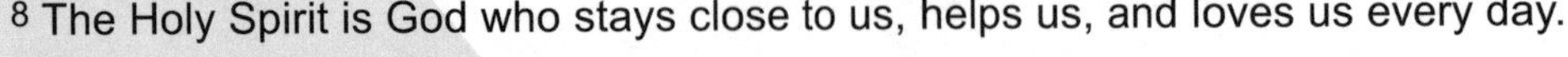

8 The Holy Spirit is God who stays close to us, helps us, and loves us every day.

The Holy Spirit never gets tired of being with God's children. He never leaves. He never forgets. He never stops loving.

He knows your name. He knows your thoughts. He knows your questions. He knows your dreams.

And He cares about all of them.

The Holy Spirit is God's presence walking beside us every day.

26. The Spirit Helps Us Understand God

Sometimes God feels very big. Sometimes the Bible feels hard to understand. We may read a story and wonder what it really means. We may read a verse and not know why it matters. When this happens, we do not need to feel worried. This is when the Holy Spirit helps us.

The Holy Spirit is our teacher. He teaches us in a kind and patient way. He does not rush us. He does not get upset when we are confused. He is happy when we want to learn about God.

Think about learning to ride a bike. At first, it feels hard. You may fall. You may feel unsure. But someone helps you. They hold the bike. They encourage you. The Holy Spirit helps us learn about God in the same gentle way.

The Spirit helps us understand who God is. He helps us see that God is loving, kind, strong, and faithful. He helps us know that God is close to us, even when we cannot see Him.

The Spirit helps us understand why God loves us. God does not love us because we are perfect. God loves us because we are His children. The Holy Spirit helps our hearts believe this, especially when we feel sad or make mistakes.

The Spirit also helps us understand Jesus. He helps us see that Jesus cared for people, healed people, forgave people, and loved children. He helps us understand that Jesus died and rose again so we could be close to God.

Without the Holy Spirit, the Bible can feel like just a book. With the Holy Spirit, the Bible feels alive. It feels like God is talking kindly to us.

For example, when you read about Jesus calming the storm, the Spirit helps you see that God can calm your fears too. When you read about the lost sheep, the Spirit helps you know that God cares about you when you feel forgotten.

Sometimes we do not understand right away. That is okay. Learning takes time. The Holy Spirit is patient, just like a teacher who explains again and again.

The Spirit also helps us know what is right and wrong. He gently reminds us to tell the truth, to be kind, and to forgive. He does not shout. He guides quietly inside our hearts.

For example, when you feel like lying but choose to tell the truth, the Spirit is helping you. When you want to be mean but choose to be kind, the Spirit is helping you.

The Spirit helps us understand ourselves too. He helps us see our mistakes without feeling useless. He helps us see our good choices without feeling proud.

When you feel sorry for doing something wrong, the Spirit is helping you. When you want to try again, the Spirit is helping you.

The Spirit reminds us that God still loves us when we fail. He reminds us that we always belong to God. He reminds us that we are never alone.

Every time you pray and say, "God, please help me understand," the Holy Spirit listens. He is happy to help you. He is gentle with your heart.

The Holy Spirit is the best teacher because He teaches us with love. And when He teaches us, we do not just learn about God. We begin to know God better.

That is the beautiful work of the Holy Spirit in our lives.

27. The Spirit Changes Our Hearts

The Holy Spirit does not only teach our minds. He also changes our hearts [9].

Our hearts are where we feel love, anger, joy, fear, and hope. Our hearts are where we choose how to act.

Sometimes our hearts want to be selfish. Sometimes our hearts want to be angry. Sometimes our hearts want to hide.

The Holy Spirit gently works inside us to change those desires.

He helps us want to love instead of hate.
He helps us want to forgive instead of stay angry.
He helps us want to be honest instead of hide.

This change does not happen all at once. It happens slowly, like a seed growing into a tree.

We may not see the change every day, but over time, we notice we are becoming kinder, gentler, and braver.

When you feel sorry after doing something wrong, the Spirit is helping you.
When you choose to forgive, the Spirit is helping you.
When you choose to tell the truth, the Spirit is helping you.

The Spirit never gives up on us. Even when we fail many times, He keeps helping us.

He never says, "I'm done with you."
He always says, "Let's try again."
He reminds us that God still loves us.
He reminds us that we are still God's children.

The Spirit changes us from the inside so our outside actions can slowly change too.

This is how God grows us.

---

[9] Your heart is the place inside you where you feel love, sadness, happiness, and choose to be kind.

28. The Fruit of the Spirit

The Bible tells us that the Holy Spirit grows fruit in our lives. This fruit is not something we can eat. It is goodness that grows inside our hearts. Just like a tree needs time, water, and sunlight to grow fruit, our hearts need God's Spirit to grow good things.

The fruit of the Spirit[10] is love, joy, peace, patience, kindness, goodness, faithfulness, gentleness, and self-control. These are not rules we must force ourselves to follow. They are signs that God is working inside us. They show that His Spirit is helping us grow.

Love helps us care about others. It helps us forgive, share, and show kindness. Joy helps us remember that God is with us, even when life feels hard. Peace helps our hearts feel calm and safe. Patience helps us wait without getting angry. Kindness helps us treat people gently. Goodness helps us choose what is right. Faithfulness helps us stay loyal and trusting. Gentleness helps us speak softly and act carefully. Self-control helps us stop and think before we act.

We cannot grow this fruit by ourselves. We need the Holy Spirit to help us. He works quietly in our hearts every day. Sometimes we do not notice the change right away, but God is still working.

Some fruit grows faster than others. You might be very kind but still learning patience. You might forgive easily but still struggle with self-control. That is okay. God is not angry with us. He is patient and loving while we grow.

Fruit takes time. A tree does not hurry, and God does not hurry us. Small changes are still important. Every kind choice, every gentle word, every honest action is fruit growing in your heart.

Sometimes you may feel like you are not growing at all. But God sees your heart. He sees your effort. He sees your desire to love. And He is happy with you.

When people see kindness, peace, and patience in you, they are really seeing God's Spirit at work. Your life becomes a quiet picture of God's love.

The fruit of the Spirit shows that God is living in us, caring for us, and helping us become more like Him, one gentle step at a time.

---

[10] This means the Holy Spirit helps good things grow inside your heart, like love and kindness.

29. The Gifts of the Spirit

The Holy Spirit also gives gifts to God's people. These gifts are special abilities that help us serve others and show God's love. They are not toys, trophies, or rewards for being perfect. They are loving tools that God places in our hearts so we can help others.

Some people are good at teaching. They explain things in ways that make sense. Some people are good at helping. They notice when someone needs a hand. Some people are good at listening. They make others feel safe to talk. Some people are good at encouraging. They use kind words to give hope. Some people are good at leading. They help groups work together. Some people are good at praying. They remember others when they talk to God. Some people are good at caring. They notice pain and bring comfort.

No one gets every gift. God did not make us all the same. He loves differences. Just like a garden needs many kinds of flowers, God's family needs many kinds of people. Each person has something special to offer.

Your gift matters. Even if your gift feels small, it is important. Helping quietly matters. Smiling kindly matters. Sharing gently matters. Listening patiently matters. Holding someone's hand matters. Saying "I care" matters.

The Spirit gives gifts so God's family can love each other better. When one person teaches, another learns. When one person helps, another feels supported. When one person listens, another feels understood. When one person encourages, another feels brave.

Gifts are not for showing off. They are not for trying to look better than others. Gifts are for serving. Gifts are for loving. Gifts are for building others up.

When we use our gifts kindly, we show God's heart. People may not see God with their eyes, but they can see His love through our actions.

The Holy Spirit also helps us use our gifts in the right way. He teaches us to stay humble. This means we remember that our gifts come from God. We stay thankful, not proud. We stay gentle, not bossy.

Sometimes we may not know what our gifts are yet. That is okay. God shows us slowly. As we grow, we begin to see what we enjoy doing and how we like helping others. The Spirit guides us gently.

Sometimes our gifts change as we grow. God keeps working in our hearts and teaching us new ways to serve.

The Spirit teaches us that no gift is too small. Cleaning, helping, sharing, praying, listening, teaching, and caring all matter. Every loving action is important to God.

And every child matters to God.

UNIT 5 — God Saves Us

Welcome to Unit 5! This unit is about one of the most comforting truths in the whole Christian faith: God saves us. That means when our hearts feel heavy, messy, or far away—God does not watch from a distance. He comes close. He reaches for us with love, and He brings us home.

In these pages, you will learn what it means to be saved. Being saved is like being pulled to safety when you cannot rescue yourself. But even more, it is God rescuing your heart—washing away sin, taking away shame, and giving you a fresh start. Saved does not mean "perfect." It means forgiven, loved, and helped. It means you belong to God's family, not because you earned it, but because God wanted you.

Unit 5 also explains why we need saving. Even when we can do good things, something inside us is still broken. We all make wrong choices sometimes. We all hurt others sometimes. We all feel fear, guilt, or pride. This is what the Bible calls sin. Sin makes hearts heavy and relationships hard. And it is something we cannot fully fix by ourselves. That is why God's rescue is not an extra thing—it is something our hearts truly need.

Then this unit gives the hopeful answer: Jesus is the only Savior. Many people can teach, help, or encourage—but only Jesus can forgive sin, heal hearts, and bring us back to God. He is strong enough to save because He is God, and close enough to understand because He became human. He did not come to blame us. He came to carry what we could not carry and to love us back into safety.

You will also learn how we come back to God: by turning back (repentance) and trusting Jesus. Turning back is not just feeling sorry—it is choosing God's way again with His help. Trusting Jesus is letting Him hold your heart the way a loving parent holds a child's hand. You do not need big words or perfect understanding. You just need a willing heart.

Unit 5 shows what happens next: new life in Christ. God begins changing us gently from the inside, like a seed growing. We still learn. We still make mistakes. But now we are not alone. We are loved, guided, and helped as we grow.

And finally, this unit ends with a truth that makes hearts feel safe: God keeps His children forever. His love is not on-and-off. He does not let go when you stumble. He holds you tighter. Your story is safe in His hands.

As you read Unit 5, go slowly. Let the message sink deep:

God saves because He is good.
God saves because He loves.

And God saves to bring you close—today and forever.

30. What Does It Mean to Be Saved?

Imagine you are walking near a deep river and you slip. The water is cold and strong, and you cannot stand up by yourself. Then someone reaches out, holds your hand, and pulls you to safety. You are no longer in danger. You are safe. That is a small picture of what it means to be saved.

Being saved does not only mean being rescued from water or fire. It means being rescued in our hearts. It means God helping us when we cannot fix ourselves.

God made people to live close to Him, to love Him, and to enjoy His goodness. But because of wrong choices, people began to feel far from God. They felt afraid, ashamed, and broken inside. They still tried to do good things, but their hearts were hurting. They needed help.

To be saved means God comes to help us come back to Him.

Being saved means our sins are forgiven. Sin is when we choose our own way instead of God's way. When we are saved, God washes our hearts clean. He does not keep a list of our mistakes. He gives us a fresh start.

Being saved also means we are not alone anymore. God becomes close to us again. We are not lost children. We are welcomed children. We belong to God's family.

Some children think being saved means becoming perfect. But that is not true. Being saved does not mean we never make mistakes again. It means we are loved even when we do. It means God stays with us while we grow.

Being saved is like being adopted into a loving family. You are not just helped once and forgotten. You are chosen and kept.

Being saved is also like having a broken toy fixed. The toy is still the same toy, but now it works again. God does not throw us away. He fixes our hearts and helps us work the way we were meant to work.

Being saved means our hearts begin to change. We start to want to love. We start to want to forgive. We start to want to do what is right. Not because we are forced, but because God's love is growing inside us.

Being saved also means we have hope. We know our story does not end with sadness. We know God is with us now and forever.

Some people think being saved is only for grown-ups. But children can be saved too. God loves children. He listens to their prayers. He welcomes their trust. He holds their hearts gently.

To be saved means trusting that Jesus loves you, forgives you, and wants you with Him.

You do not need to understand everything.
You do not need to be perfect.
You do not need to be big or smart.

You only need to trust that God loves you and wants to save you.

When you are saved, God does not just change your future. He changes your today. He gives you peace when you are afraid. He gives you comfort when you are sad. He gives you strength when you feel weak.

Being saved means you are never alone again.
Being saved means you are deeply loved.
Being saved means God is holding your life in His hands.

And the most beautiful part is this: God does not save people because they are already good. He saves people because He is good.

To be saved means to be found, forgiven, loved, and kept by God forever.

And once you understand that, you begin to realize something wonderful. Being saved is not the end of the story. It is the beginning of a brand new life with God.

31. Why We Need Saving

At first, some children wonder, "Why do we even need to be saved?" After all, we can laugh, play, learn, and do many good things. We can help others, share, and say kind words. So why would we need God to rescue us?

The answer is gentle and honest. We need saving because something inside our hearts is not working the way God first made it to work.

God created people to love Him, trust Him, and love one another. He wanted our hearts to be full of goodness, truth, and kindness. But over time, people began to choose selfishness, lies, and hurt instead of love and truth. These wrong choices are called sin. Sin is not only very big, bad actions. It is also small choices, like refusing to forgive, wanting to be first all the time, or not caring about others. These choices may seem small, but they slowly hurt our hearts.

Sin makes hearts feel heavy. It makes people feel ashamed. It makes people hide. It makes people try to fix themselves but fail again and again. Even when we want to be kind, we sometimes choose wrong. Even when we want to tell the truth, we sometimes lie. Even when we want to love, we sometimes hurt.

That is why we need saving.

We need saving because our hearts cannot heal themselves. Just like a broken arm needs a doctor, a broken heart needs God. We cannot clean our own sin away. We cannot make ourselves perfectly right again. We need someone who loves us enough to help us.

We also need saving because sin separates us from God. Not because God stops loving us, but because our hearts stop trusting Him. It is like when a child runs away from a parent. The parent still loves the child, but the child feels far away. God wants to bring us back close to Him.

We need saving because sin does not only hurt us. It hurts others too. It breaks friendships. It breaks families. It breaks peace. God does not want us to live in broken relationships. He wants to heal them.

We also need saving because the world is full of pain, sickness, and sadness. God never wanted the world to be this way. He wants to fix it, and He starts by fixing hearts.

Some children think saving is only for very bad people. But saving is for everyone. Even good children need saving, because no one loves perfectly. No one is kind all the time. No one is brave all the time. We all need God's help.

Needing saving does not mean we are terrible. It means we are human. It means we are loved enough for God to want to help us.

God does not say, "You are too broken."
He says, "You are too loved to be left broken."

God does not say, "Fix yourself first."
He says, "Come to Me and I will help you."

God does not save us because we deserve it. He saves us because He loves us.

When we understand why we need saving, we stop pretending we are perfect. We start trusting God. We stop hiding. We start coming close to Him.

We realize that God is not our enemy. He is our rescuer.

We need saving so our hearts can be clean again.
We need saving so we can feel close to God again.
We need saving so love can grow inside us again.

And when we understand that, we begin to ask a very important question:

If we need saving so much, who can save us?

That beautiful answer comes next.

32. Jesus Is the Only Savior

When children hear about saving, they sometimes wonder, "Can anyone save us?" Maybe a very good teacher, a strong hero, or a kind leader? Many people in history have tried to help the world, and some have done good things. But only one person can truly save hearts and bring people back to God. That person is Jesus.

Jesus is the only Savior because He is the only one who is both God and human. He understands our lives because He lived like us. He understands our hearts because He feels like us. But He also has God's power to forgive, heal, and give new life. No one else in history is like that.

Other people can teach us how to live better. They can tell us to be kind, honest, and brave. But they cannot take away our sin. They cannot clean our hearts. They cannot bring us back to God. Only Jesus can do that.

Jesus is the only Savior because He lived a perfect life. He never chose wrong. He never hurt others with selfishness. He never turned away from love. This means He did not need saving Himself. Because He was perfect, He could save others.

Jesus is also the only Savior because He gave His life for us. He did not run away from pain. He did not protect Himself. He chose to suffer so we could be forgiven. He took our wrong choices and carried them with love. No one else has ever done that.

Some people think, "I can be good enough by myself." But being saved is not about being good enough. It is about being loved enough. Jesus did not come because we were already perfect. He came because we needed help.

Other people can forgive small mistakes. Jesus can forgive the heart. Other people can change our behavior for a while. Jesus can change us from the inside. Other people can promise to stay, but only Jesus can stay forever.

Jesus is the only Savior because He did not stay dead. He rose again. This shows that His love is stronger than death, stronger than sin, and stronger than fear. A Savior who is alive can still help, still listen, and still love.

Sometimes children ask, "Why can't I save myself?" The answer is simple and gentle. We cannot lift ourselves when we are fallen. We cannot clean our hearts completely. We cannot make ourselves perfect. But Jesus can.

Jesus does not save us by pushing us. He saves us by holding us. He does not save us by shouting. He saves us by loving us. He does not save us by forcing us. He saves us by inviting us.

Jesus is not one of many saviors. He is the Savior. He is the bridge between God and people. He is the door back to God's heart.

This does not mean other people are not important. It means they need saving too. Everyone needs Jesus.

Jesus is the only Savior because only He can forgive sin, heal hearts, and give new life. Only He can bring us fully back to God. Only He can promise forever.

When we trust Jesus, we are not trusting just a teacher. We are trusting our Savior. We are trusting the One who knows us completely and loves us perfectly.

Jesus is the only Savior, not because God wanted only one way, but because God wanted the best way. And that best way is love.

And when we understand that Jesus is the only Savior, we begin to wonder something very important.

How do we come back to God?

That is what we will learn next.

33. Turning Back to God

Sometimes you make a wrong choice. Maybe you said something unkind. Maybe you didn't listen. Maybe you did something you knew was not right. When that happens, you might feel funny inside. Your heart may feel heavy. You might want to hide or stay quiet. That feeling is your heart telling you it needs God again.

Turning back to God means choosing to come close to Him instead of staying far away. It means you remember that God loves you and wants to help you.

God never stops loving you. Not ever. Even when you make mistakes. Even when you choose the wrong thing. His love does not change. But sometimes we stop listening to Him. Sometimes we want to do things our own way. That is when our hearts drift away. Turning back to God means stopping, thinking, and choosing to go back to Him.

You do not have to be scared to turn back to God. You just have to be honest. You can say, "God, I made a mistake. Please help me." God is not surprised. He already knows. And He is ready to forgive you right away.

Think about when you break a toy. You can hide it, or you can bring it to a grown-up to help fix it. Turning back to God is like bringing Him the broken toy. God does not get angry. He does not yell. He gently helps fix what is broken inside your heart.

The Bible calls turning back to God "repentance.[11]" That is a big word, but it means something simple. It means you turn around. You stop going the wrong way and start going God's way again. It is not only saying "sorry." It is choosing to try again with God's help.

When you turn back to God, He does not push you away. He does not keep reminding you of your mistake. He forgives you. He welcomes you. He is happy you came back. Just like a parent feels happy when a child comes home, God feels happy when you come back to Him.

Turning back to God does not mean you will never make another mistake. You are still learning. God knows that. He is patient with you. He teaches you little by little. He helps you grow every day.

---

[11] Repentance means saying, "I'm sorry," and choosing to go back to God's way with His help.

Sometimes you may feel proud and think, “I’m fine.” But God wants you to be honest. He wants you to talk to Him. He wants you to tell Him when you are scared, sad, confused, or sorry. When you do, your heart feels lighter.

The heavy feelings start to go away. Guilt gets smaller. Fear gets quieter. Shame starts to heal. God fills your heart with peace and love again.

You can turn back to God anytime.
You can turn back when you are unkind.

You can turn back when you lie.
You can turn back when you forget to love.
You can turn back when you make a bad choice.

God never gets tired of forgiving you. He never says, “That’s enough.” He always keeps His heart open for you.

Even adults have to turn back to God again and again. Everyone does. That does not mean you are bad. It means you are human and still learning. And God loves people who are learning.

God is like a loving Father who always keeps the door open. He is watching for you, not to punish you, but to hug you close again.

When you turn back to God, you remember something very important:
You belong to Him.
You are loved.
And you are never too far away to be forgiven.

34. Trusting Jesus

Trusting Jesus means believing that He loves you, listens to you, and wants what is best for you. It is like trusting a loving parent to hold your hand when you cross a busy street. You may not understand everything about the road, but you know the parent will keep you safe. Trusting Jesus is letting Him hold your heart and take care of it.

Trust is not something we do only with our minds. It is something we do with our hearts. When you trust Jesus, you believe that He is kind, even when life feels hard. You believe that He forgives you when you make mistakes. You believe that He is with you, even when you cannot see Him. You believe that He cares about every little part of your life.

Some children think trusting Jesus means never feeling afraid or sad. But that is not true. Trusting Jesus means you bring your fear and sadness to Him instead of hiding them. You can tell Him everything. You can tell Him when you are scared, when you are hurt, and when you are confused. He is not tired of listening. He is happy when you talk to Him.

Trusting Jesus also means believing His words. When Jesus says God loves you, you believe it. When Jesus says you are forgiven, you accept it. When Jesus says He will never leave you, you hold onto that promise. Trust grows when you remember what Jesus has said and let His words stay in your heart.

Sometimes trusting Jesus is easy, like when you feel happy and safe. Other times it is harder, like when you feel confused, lonely, or hurt. But Jesus is the same in both moments. He does not change. He is steady, gentle, and faithful. He stays with you no matter how you feel.

Trusting Jesus does not mean you understand everything. It means you choose to believe even when you do not understand. A child may not understand how a plane flies, but still trusts the pilot. In the same way, you may not understand everything about life, but you can trust Jesus to guide you and protect you.

When you trust Jesus, you begin to follow Him. You try to love like He loves. You try to forgive like He forgives. You try to be kind because you know He is kind. Trust slowly changes the way you think, the way you speak, and the way you treat others.

Trusting Jesus also helps you when you fail. Instead of running away in shame, you come back to Him. You know He will forgive you and help you try again. Trust teaches you that Jesus is not only your Savior, but also your helper, teacher, and friend.

Trust grows little by little. It grows when you pray. It grows when you hear Bible stories. It grows when you see kindness. It grows when you remember how Jesus has helped you before. God is patient while your trust grows. He never rushes you.

Some children worry that they are not good enough to trust Jesus. But Jesus never asks you to be good enough. He only asks you to come. Trusting Jesus is not about being perfect. It is about believing that He is perfect in love and care for you.

When you trust Jesus, you are not giving Him just a small part of your heart. You are giving Him your whole heart. And when you do, He keeps it safely. He protects it with love, mercy, and grace.

Trusting Jesus means choosing love instead of fear, hope instead of worry, and faith instead of hiding. It means knowing that you are never walking alone. Jesus walks with you every day, even when you do not notice.

And when you begin to trust Jesus more and more, something wonderful starts to happen inside you. Your heart begins to feel lighter. Your mind begins to feel calmer. Your spirit begins to feel new. That is the beautiful power of trusting Jesus.

35. New Life in Christ

When someone trusts Jesus, something very special begins inside them. It is called new life in Christ. This new life does not mean we suddenly look different on the outside. It means our hearts begin to change on the inside.

New life in Christ is like planting a small seed in the soil. At first, you cannot see much. But under the ground, the seed is growing. In the same way, when Jesus comes into our hearts, He starts growing new love, new hope, and new kindness inside us.

Before new life, hearts often feel heavy with guilt, fear, or worry. After new life begins, hearts start to feel lighter. We begin to understand that we are forgiven. We begin to feel that we belong. We begin to know that God is close.

New life in Christ does not make us perfect. We still make mistakes. We still feel sad sometimes. We still learn slowly. But now we are not alone while we grow. Jesus walks with us and helps us change little by little.

New life in Christ is like learning to walk again, but this time with help. When we fall, Jesus helps us stand. When we are tired, Jesus gives us strength. When we are confused, Jesus guides us.

This new life also changes the way we see others. We start to care more. We start to forgive more easily. We start to notice people who feel lonely. We start to want to do what is right, not because we are forced, but because love is growing in us.

New life in Christ also changes the way we see ourselves. We stop thinking we are only our mistakes. We start believing we are loved. We stop feeling like we must hide. We start feeling safe to be honest.

Imagine wearing dirty clothes for a long time and then putting on clean ones. You still look like you, but you feel fresh and new. That is what new life in Christ feels like in the heart.

God does not take away our personality. He does not erase who we are. He makes who we are better. He keeps our laughter, our dreams, and our uniqueness, but He fills them with love.

New life in Christ also gives us a new family. We become part of God's family. Other believers become our brothers and sisters in faith. We are no longer walking alone.

This new life gives us new hope for the future. We know that our story does not end with sadness. We know God is working in us. We know He has good plans.

Sometimes children wonder, "How do I know I have new life?" The answer is simple. If you trust Jesus, love Him, and want to follow Him, new life has already begun in you, even if you cannot see it clearly yet.

New life in Christ is not loud like fireworks. It is gentle like a growing plant. It grows every day when we pray, learn, forgive, and love.

God is patient with our new life. He does not rush us. He celebrates every small step. He is happy when we try.

New life in Christ means we are not who we used to be. And we are not yet who we will be. We are growing in love.

And this beautiful new life is not something God will ever take away from us. That is why the next truth is so comforting to learn.

God keeps us forever.

36. God Keeps Us Forever

When children love something special, they sometimes worry about losing it. They worry a favorite toy might break, or a friend might go away. In the same way, some children wonder, "If God loves me now, will He always love me?" The beautiful answer is yes. God keeps His children forever.

God's love is not like a light that turns on and off. It is like the sun. Even when clouds cover it, the sun is still there. In the same way, even when we make mistakes or feel far from God, His love does not disappear.

When God saves us, He does not say, "I will love you only if you behave perfectly." He says, "You are My child now." And once someone becomes God's child, they belong to Him forever.

Think about a parent holding a child's hand while walking. Even if the child stumbles, the parent does not let go. The parent holds tighter. God does the same with us. When we feel weak, He holds us. When we feel scared, He stays close. When we feel unsure, He does not leave.

God keeps us not because we are strong, but because He is strong.
God keeps us not because we never fail, but because His love never fails.
God keeps us because He promised to.

Sometimes children think God might stop loving them when they do something wrong. But God already knows every mistake we will make, and He still chose to love us. His love is bigger than our failures.

When we fall, God lifts us.
When we forget, God remembers.
When we feel lost, God finds us.

God keeping us forever means we are never alone. Even when we cannot see Him, He is with us. Even when we do not feel brave, He is protecting us. Even when we are sleeping, He is watching over us.

God keeping us forever also means our future is safe. No matter what happens in life, God is holding our story. He is guiding our days. He is preparing good things for us.

Sometimes children worry about growing up. They worry about changes, new places, and new people. God keeping us forever means we never face the future alone. God goes with us into every tomorrow.

God keeping us forever does not mean life will never be hard. It means we will never be alone in hard times. It means God will always be close to our hearts.

God keeping us forever also means His love will never get tired. He never says, "I have loved you enough." He never says, "I am done with you." His love has no ending.

When Jesus promised to stay with His people, He meant it. He promised to be with us always. Not just on good days. Not just when we pray. Not just when we behave well. Always.

God keeping us forever means we belong to Him today, tomorrow, and forever.

It means our hearts are safe in His hands.
It means our story is wrapped in His love.
It means nothing can separate us from Him.

God does not keep us like something He might lose. He keeps us like something He treasures.

And because God keeps us forever, we can live with peaceful hearts, knowing that we are loved, protected, and never forgotten.

We are God's children.

And God never lets go of His children.

UNIT 6 — God's Family: The Church

Welcome to Unit 6! In this unit, you will learn something warm and comforting: God saves us into a family. He does not rescue us and then send us back alone. He brings us into a place where we can belong, grow, and be loved. That family is called the church.

Many children think church means a building. Buildings can be beautiful, and they can help people gather—but the church is much bigger than walls. The church is people: people who love Jesus and are learning to follow Him together. Wherever God's children pray, learn, forgive, help, and love—that is the church.

In Unit 6, you will discover why God wants His children to meet together. Just like a fire burns brighter when sticks are close, faith grows stronger when hearts are together. When we gather, we remember we belong. We find courage when we feel weak. We find comfort when we feel sad. We learn we are not the only ones who wonder, struggle, or need help.

This unit will also explain special family moments like baptism and communion—simple, beautiful ways God helps us remember Jesus' love and promises. You will learn about worship and prayer, not just as things we do on one day of the week, but as ways we love God with our whole lives. And you will see that every person has a place in God's family, because God gives each one gifts to serve with love.

Unit 6 is also honest: the church is not perfect, because people are not perfect. Sometimes people misunderstand each other or make mistakes. But God does not give up on His family. He uses the church to teach patience, healing, and forgiveness—so love can grow stronger.

Most of all, this unit will help you feel the truth in your bones: you are needed. Your prayers matter. Your kindness matters. Your small acts of love matter. In God's family, no one is extra and no one is invisible.

As you read Unit 6, let your heart rest in this:
The church is not a building you enter.
It is a family you belong to.
And with God's family, you never have to walk alone.

37. What Is the Church?

When many children hear the word “church,” they imagine a building with tall walls, colorful windows, rows of chairs, and songs playing inside. Some think of a stage, a cross, or a person speaking at the front. These things can be part of church, but they are not what church truly is. God teaches us that the church is not only a place you visit. The church is something alive and special.

The church is people. It is God’s family. The church is made of people who love Jesus and want to follow Him. When they pray together, learn together, forgive each other, and help each other, they are being the church. Even when they laugh together, cry together, or share food together, they are living as God’s family.

People can meet in many different places. Some meet in large buildings with bells and towers. Some meet in small homes with only a few chairs. Some meet in schools, parks, or even under trees. God is happy in all these places, because the church is not made of walls or floors. It is made of hearts that love Him.

God created the church because He knew people were not meant to live alone. He made humans to love, talk, share, and grow together. Just like birds fly better in groups and fish swim better in schools, people grow better when they are part of a caring family. God wants His children to walk together, not by themselves.

In God’s family, everyone matters. Children matter. Teenagers matter. Adults matter. Grandparents matter. People who talk a lot matter. People who speak softly matter. People who understand many things about God matter. People who are still learning matter. God does not look at age, size, or strength. He looks at hearts.

The church is a place where people can feel safe. When someone is sad, others can listen and care. When someone is afraid, others can pray and encourage them. When someone feels lonely, others can remind them that they belong. God wants no one in His family to feel forgotten.

The church is also a place of joy. People sing together, smile together, celebrate together, and thank God together. Joy grows when it is shared. God loves to see His children happy and thankful together.

The church teaches people how to love better. Love is not only about kind words. Love is about patience, helping, listening, and forgiving. In church, people learn how to care even when it is hard. They learn how to stay gentle even when they are upset. They learn how to choose kindness instead of anger.

The church is not perfect, because people are not perfect. Sometimes people misunderstand each other. Sometimes they forget to be kind. Sometimes they make mistakes. But God does not give up on His family. Instead, He uses these moments to teach forgiveness, patience, and healing.

Forgiveness is very important in the church. When someone says sorry, God wants others to forgive. When someone is hurt, God wants comfort to follow. Forgiveness helps hearts feel lighter and happier again.

The church is also a place for learning. People learn about God's love, God's promises, and God's ways. They learn stories about Jesus, about kindness, about courage, and about faith. Learning helps people grow stronger inside.

Children are very important in the church. Jesus loves children deeply. He listens to their prayers, sees their kindness, and smiles at their faith. Children remind adults how to trust God simply and honestly.

The church is not about being famous, rich, or powerful. It is not about wearing special clothes or saying fancy words. It is about loving God with your heart and loving people with your actions. God cares more about love than about anything else.

Jesus loves the church very much. He calls it His body. This means every person is like a part of Him. Just as a body needs every hand, foot, and eye, the church needs every person. No one is extra. No one is useless. Everyone has a place.

When someone helps, the church grows stronger. When someone prays, the church grows closer to God. When someone forgives, the church grows kinder. When someone believes, the church grows brighter.

The church is also a place for hope. When life feels hard, the church reminds people that God is still good. When days feel dark, the church reminds people that God's light is still shining.

God's family is not only for one day of the week. The church continues at home, at school, at work, and everywhere people show love, kindness, and faith.

Being part of the church means you are never alone. God walks with you. His family walks with you. You belong. You are loved. You are needed.

No matter how small you feel, God sees you. No matter how young you are, God values you. No matter how much you still need to learn, God welcomes you.

The church is not a building you enter. It is a family you belong to. It is a place where hearts grow, love spreads, and God's goodness shines.

And when you are part of that family, you carry God's love wherever you go. When you are part of the church, you are part of God's family forever.

38. Why We Meet Together

God knows that hearts grow stronger when they are together. That is why people who love Jesus meet together.

When we meet together, we remember that we belong. We see faces that care. We hear voices that pray. We feel less alone in the world.

Meeting together helps us learn. We hear Bible stories. We ask questions. We listen to others. We learn that we are not the only ones who struggle or wonder.

Meeting together also gives courage. When we see others trusting God, it helps us trust Him too. When we see others forgive, it helps us forgive. When we see others love, it helps us love.

God knows that faith grows best when it is shared. A fire burns brighter when many sticks are together. In the same way, faith grows brighter when people are together.

Meeting together is not only about sitting quietly. It is about singing, praying, listening, helping, and caring. It is about hearts growing, not just bodies sitting.

Children do not need to be perfect at church. Church is not for perfect people. It is for learning people. God welcomes children with energy, questions, and curious hearts.

When we meet together, we remind each other that God is real, God is kind, and God is near. We remember that we are loved and not forgotten.

Meeting together does not make us God's children. It helps us remember that we already are.

When we meet together, we also learn how to help each other. We learn to share, to wait our turn, and to be kind even when it is hard. We learn that small actions, like a smile or a hug, can make someone's day brighter. God uses little hearts to do big things.

Meeting together reminds us that everyone is important. Big people and small people both matter to God. Every voice, every prayer, and every song is special to Him. When children sing, God listens with joy.

Sometimes we feel shy, tired, or unsure. But when we come together, God gently fills us with peace. He reminds us that we are never alone.

Church is like a family that helps each other grow. We grow in love. We grow in faith. We grow in hope. And we grow best when we grow together, with God smiling over us all.

39. Baptism and Communion

Baptism and communion are special ways God helps His family remember His love and His promises. They are not just traditions or activities. They are gentle reminders that God is close, that Jesus loves us, and that we belong to Him.

Baptism is when a person is gently placed in water and then lifted out again. The water does not magically change the person, but it shows something beautiful. It shows that God has forgiven their sins and given them new life. Going into the water is like saying goodbye to the old life, and coming out of the water is like saying hello to a new life with Jesus.

Baptism is like washing dirty hands. When your hands are dirty, you wash them to make them clean again. In the same way, baptism shows that God has washed our hearts with His love and forgiveness. It tells the world, “I belong to Jesus now, and I want to follow Him.”

Baptism does not make God love someone more. God already loves every person completely, even before baptism. Baptism is not something we do to earn God’s love. It is something we do because we already have His love. It is a happy way to show trust and thankfulness.

Communion is another special gift from God. When people take communion, they eat a small piece of bread and drink from a cup. These are simple things, but they remind us of something very important. The bread reminds us of Jesus’ body, and the cup reminds us of His love and sacrifice.

Communion helps us remember that Jesus gave Himself so we could be close to God. It reminds us that Jesus chose love, even when it was hard. It reminds us that we are forgiven and welcomed into God’s family.

Communion is not about being hungry or thirsty. It is about remembering and thanking. It is about slowing down and thinking about how much Jesus loves us. It is about feeling close to Him in our hearts.

When people take communion together, they also remember that they are part of one family. They are not alone. They belong to God and to each other.

Baptism and communion both help people remember God's story. They remind us where we came from, who we belong to, and where we are going. They remind us that God saves, God loves, and God stays.

These special moments help hearts stay soft, thankful, and trusting. They help children and grown-ups remember that following Jesus is not just about rules, but about love, grace, and a relationship with God.

Through baptism and communion, God gently reminds His family, again and again, "You are Mine, you are loved, and you are never alone."

40. Worship and Prayer

Worship is how we show God that we love Him with our whole hearts. We worship when we sing, pray, listen, obey, and thank Him. Worship is not only something we do in church. We can worship God when we help others, when we tell the truth, and when we choose kindness. Worship is love shown in action. It is a way of living that honors God in both big and small moments. Every good choice we make can become an act of worship when it is done with a loving and grateful heart.

Worship also teaches us to focus on God instead of only on ourselves. When we worship, we remember who God is and how much He loves us. We remember His goodness, His mercy, and His faithfulness. Worship fills our hearts with peace and reminds us that God is greater than any problem we face.

Prayer is how we talk with God. We can talk to Him like we talk to a loving parent or a close friend. We can tell Him about our happy moments and our sad moments. We can talk to Him about school, friends, fears, and dreams. God listens to every word, even the ones we only think in our hearts. Prayer helps us remember that God cares about every part of our lives, not just the important or serious parts.

Prayer also helps us make better choices. When we pray, we invite God to guide our thoughts and actions. We learn to be patient, humble, and thankful. Prayer gives us strength when we feel weak and hope when we feel unsure.

We do not need special or perfect words. God understands whispers, tears, laughter, and quiet thoughts. He understands when we are thankful, confused, tired, or joyful. Prayer reminds us that we are never alone. Worship reminds us that God is always good. Even when life feels difficult, prayer and worship help us trust that God is still with us.

When we worship and pray together, our hearts grow closer to God and closer to each other. We learn to love, forgive, and encourage one another. Worship teaches us gratitude, and prayer teaches us trust. Together, they help us grow stronger in faith and kinder in spirit.

Worship and prayer are not about being perfect. They are about being honest. God wants our real thoughts, real feelings, and real love. When we worship and pray every day, we build a deeper relationship with Him. We begin to see His love in our lives, in our families, and in the world around us.

In worship, we lift our hearts to God. In prayer, we place our hearts in His hands. Both remind us that we are deeply loved, carefully guided, and never forgotten.

41. Serving With Our Gifts

God gives every person special gifts. These gifts are not always big or loud. Some people are good at helping. Some are good at teaching. Some are good at listening. Some are good at drawing. Some are good at making others smile. Every gift is important. No gift is too small, and no gift is useless. God carefully chose each gift for each person, knowing exactly how it could be used to bring good into the world. Even talents we may not notice right away can become powerful when they are used with love.

God did not give gifts so people could show off. He gave gifts so people could help. When we use our gifts, we make God's family stronger. We help others feel loved, safe, and important. Our gifts are meant to lift people up, not to make ourselves look better. When we serve with kindness, our gifts become tools of love that bring comfort, joy, and hope to those around us.

Even small gifts matter. A smile can make someone feel seen. A hug can make someone feel comforted. A kind word can change a sad day. God sees every loving action, even when others do not notice. Nothing done with love is ever wasted. What seems small to us can mean everything to someone else.

Sometimes we may think our gifts are not good enough. We may feel shy or unsure about using them. But God never makes mistakes. He knows that each gift has a purpose. When we use what we have, God can do great things through us.

Our gifts can be used in many places—at home, at school, in church, and in our community. When we choose to serve others with kindness, we show that our hearts belong to God. Our gifts are God's way of shining His light through us and bringing hope to the world.

42. Loving Others

Jesus said loving others is one of the most important things we can do. Love means being kind when it is easy and when it is hard. Love means being patient when others are slow. Love means forgiving when someone hurts us. Love means caring even when we feel tired. Love is not just a feeling in our hearts; it is a choice we make every day[12] through our words and actions.

Loving others is not always simple. People are different. People make mistakes. People sometimes say or do things that hurt. Sometimes they do not understand us, and sometimes we do not understand them. But Jesus teaches us to love anyway, because love has the power to heal hearts. Love can fix broken friendships, bring peace to angry moments, and give hope to those who feel alone.

Love does not mean we must agree with everything. It means we choose kindness instead of anger. It means we choose understanding instead of judging. It means we choose forgiveness instead of holding hate. Love reminds us that every person matters, even when they are difficult to love. It reminds us that everyone is learning, growing, and trying in their own way.

When we love others, we show them what God's heart looks like. Through our love, people can see God's kindness, patience, and mercy. Loving others is one of the strongest ways we can share God's love with the world. Sometimes people may never read the Bible, but they will see God through how we treat them.

Love can be shown in many simple ways. We can listen when someone needs to talk. We can help when someone is struggling. We can speak gently instead of harshly. We can include people who feel left out. We can stand up for those who are treated unfairly. These small acts of love can make a big difference in someone's life.

Loving others also means loving people who are not like us. It means loving people with different opinions, different backgrounds, and different personalities. Love helps us see that our differences do not separate us, but instead make the world more beautiful. When we love across differences, we show that God's love is for everyone.

Sometimes loving others requires courage. It takes courage to forgive when we are hurt. It takes courage to be kind when we are misunderstood. It takes courage to keep loving when we feel unappreciated. But God gives us strength to love, even when it feels difficult. He never asks us to love alone. He walks with us and helps our hearts grow.

---

[12] A choice is when you decide what to do, like choosing to be kind.

Love also begins in our own hearts. When we remember how much God loves us, it becomes easier to love others. When we feel thankful for God's forgiveness, we can forgive more easily. When we feel God's patience with us, we can become more patient with others. God's love fills us so that we can pour love into the lives of others.

Loving others does not mean we will never feel hurt or disappointed. But it means we choose to respond with grace instead of bitterness. It means we choose peace instead of revenge. It means we trust God to heal what we cannot fix by ourselves.

Love can change families, schools, friendships, and communities. Love can stop arguments. Love can build trust. Love can bring comfort to those who feel forgotten. Every loving choice we make becomes part of God's work in the world.

Jesus showed us the perfect example of love. He loved people who were ignored. He loved people who were broken. He loved people who made mistakes. He loved people who did not understand Him. His love was gentle, strong, and full of mercy. When we try to love like Jesus, we become better friends, better family members, and better followers of God.

Loving others is not always easy, but it is always worth it. Love brings light into dark places. Love brings peace into troubled hearts. Love brings hope into difficult days. When we choose love, we choose to walk in God's way.

In the end, loving others is not just something we do. It is who we are becoming. We are becoming people who reflect God's heart. We are becoming people who bring kindness into the world. And through our love, others can see that God is real, God is good, and God is full of love.

43. Sharing God's Good News

God's good news is simple and beautiful. God loves people. Jesus saves. Hearts can be made new. This good news is meant for everyone, not just grown-ups or perfect people. It is for children, families, friends, and even people who feel lonely or forgotten. God's good news tells us that no one is too small, too broken, or too far away to be loved by Him.

Sharing God's good news does not mean shouting or forcing others to listen. It means caring, helping, and speaking gently. It means showing love first, and then sharing words when the time is right. God wants His message to feel safe and kind, not scary or confusing. When we speak with love, people can hear God's heart more clearly.

We share God's good news when we forgive someone who hurt us. We share it when we help someone in need. We share it when we are kind, honest, and patient. Our actions often speak louder than our words. When we choose kindness, we are showing others what God's love looks like in real life.

Sometimes we may feel shy about sharing God's good news. We may think we are too young or not smart enough. But God loves to use children. He knows that children can share love in very special ways. A smile, a kind word, or a caring hug can open someone's heart to God's love.

We can share God's good news at school, at home, on the playground, and with our friends. We can invite others to pray with us. We can tell them that God loves them when they feel sad. We can remind them that they are important to God. Every small act of love helps spread God's good news.

When people see love, they become curious about God. When they see kindness, they begin to wonder where it comes from. When they see patience and forgiveness, they begin to feel hope. God wants His love to travel from heart to heart, and He uses His children to carry that love into the world with gentle and joyful hearts.

Sharing God's good news is not about being perfect. It is about being loving. It is about letting God's light shine through us. And when we share His good news, even in small ways, we help make the world a brighter, kinder, and happier place for everyone.

UNIT 7 — God's Forever Plan

Welcome to Unit 7! This is the last unit, and it is full of hope. In this unit, we talk about big questions that many children quietly carry in their hearts—questions about death, heaven, the future, and what God will do with His world. God is not afraid of our questions. He is gentle with them. And He wants our hearts to feel safe.

Unit 7 teaches that death is not the end of the story. When someone dies, we may feel deep sadness, and God understands those tears. But the Bible tells us that God holds people with love, and that life continues in His care. Because Jesus rose again, death is not the final word. It is not a dark wall—it is a doorway God can carry His children through.

In these pages, you will learn about heaven as God's real, joyful home—full of peace, beauty, and belonging. A place where no one is sick, scared, lonely, or unwanted. You will also learn why Christians speak carefully about hell—not to scare children, but to show that love must be chosen, and that God's heart is always invitation and rescue.

Unit 7 also reminds us of a powerful promise: Jesus will return. The world still has brokenness, but God has not forgotten it. Jesus will come again to finish His rescue story—to heal what hurts, to make wrong things right, and to gather His people into lasting peace.

Then comes one of the most beautiful truths in the whole book: God will make everything new. He will not throw His world away. He will fix it. He will heal every tear, remove fear and pain, and fill creation with joy the way it was always meant to be. God will also judge fairly—not with cruelty, but with perfect goodness—so that evil does not last forever and love can finally shine without darkness.

This unit ends with the promise every heart longs for: living forever with God. Not as a boring ending, but as real life at its best—safe, bright, joyful, and full of love. A forever home where love does not run out, where goodbyes are gone, and where God's children are finally, completely home.

As you read Unit 7, go slowly. Let your heart rest in this:
God's plan is not fear.
God's plan is not loss.
God's plan is forever love—and it ends with a world made new.

44. What Happens After We Die?

Many children quietly wonder, “What happens when someone dies?” Some feel curious. Some feel scared. Some feel sad. God knows our hearts ask these questions, and He is not upset when we ask them. He wants us to know that death is not the end of our story.

When a person dies, their body stops working, but their soul does not disappear. The Bible teaches that God holds every soul with love. Our life does not fade into nothing—it continues in God’s care.

Think about when you fall asleep at night. Your body rests, but your story does not end. In a greater way, death is like falling asleep in God’s arms and waking up in His presence.

God created people to live forever with Him. Death entered the world because of sin, but it never had the final word. Jesus defeated death by rising again. That means death is not a wall anymore—it is a doorway.

When someone who loves Jesus dies, they are not lost or alone. They are with God, who loves them more than anyone else ever could.

This does not mean we will not feel sad. God understands tears. Jesus Himself cried when someone He loved died. God does not ask us to hide our sadness, but He gives us hope because He is holding our loved ones.

The Bible does not tell us every detail about being with God after death, but it tells us enough to feel safe. God is good, gentle, and full of love. Being with Him is peaceful and joyful.

Death does not mean being forgotten. It means being remembered by God forever. It does not mean being alone—it means being welcomed home.

God promises that one day He will bring His children together again in a new world where death will be no more. That is why Christians do not see death as the end, but as the beginning of life with God.

When we think about death, we remember hope and God’s love. Our story does not end in darkness. It ends in God’s light.

45. Heaven

Heaven is not a cloudy place where people float and feel bored. Heaven is a real place[13] filled with God's presence, joy, beauty, peace, and love. It is the home God prepared for His children.

In heaven, no one is sick. No one is scared. No one feels lonely. No one feels unwanted. Every heart feels safe and whole.

Heaven is not quiet in a sad way. It is joyful in a peaceful way. People worship, laugh, rest, and enjoy being with God. They feel completely loved and completely at home.

Jesus said He is preparing a place for His people. That means heaven is not a surprise house. It is a carefully prepared home made with love.

Imagine the happiest place you can think of. Now imagine it with no pain, no fear, no fighting, no tears, and no goodbyes. Heaven is even better than that.

In heaven, people will know God fully. They will not wonder if God loves them. They will feel His love all around them. They will not feel small or forgotten. They will feel deeply known and deeply valued.

Heaven is also a place of reunion. God will bring His children together. Families, friends, and believers will be together again, but without sadness or separation.

Heaven is not about escaping the world. It is about finally living in the world God always wanted — full of love, peace, and joy.

Some children worry heaven might be boring. But God created play, laughter, colors, music, and joy. Heaven will be filled with these things in perfect ways.

Heaven is not only about rest. It is about life at its best.

And heaven is not far away in God's heart. He thinks about it when He thinks about you. He wants you there with Him forever.

Heaven reminds us that love never ends.
Heaven reminds us that God keeps His promises.
Heaven reminds us that our story is beautiful.

[13] Heaven is God's happy home where love never stops and everyone feels safe.

46. Hell

The Bible teaches that hell is a place far away from God. God is full of love, kindness, and peace. When people are far from God, they are far from those good things. God made people to be close to Him. He wanted to be their friend. He wanted to love them and care for them. But God also gave people a special gift. That gift is choice.

God never forces anyone to love Him. Love must be chosen. Love is not real if it is forced. God wants everyone to choose Him. He wants everyone to choose love, forgiveness, and life. He wants everyone to know they are special and deeply loved.

God wants people to choose kindness instead of meanness. He wants people to choose forgiveness instead of anger. He wants people to choose helping instead of hurting. God knows these choices make the world better and hearts happier.

But God also respects people's choices. Even when people choose to walk away from Him, God does not stop loving them. God never stops caring. God never stops hoping. God never stops loving.

Hell is not a place God enjoys. God does not want anyone to go there. God does not like sadness or pain. God's heart is gentle and kind. The Bible says God wants everyone to be saved and to know His love. God wants everyone to feel safe, forgiven, and welcomed.

God wants everyone to come close to Him like a child runs to a loving parent. Hell shows us that love must be freely chosen. Love is only real when someone wants to give it. God does not want robots. He wants real people with real hearts and real love.

The saddest part of hell is not fire or darkness. The saddest part is being far from God. God is where love lives. God is where joy lives. God is where peace lives. God never wanted anyone to feel alone.

That is why God sent Jesus. God sent Jesus so no one would have to be far from Him. Jesus came to show love. Jesus came to forgive. Jesus came to help people come back to God.
Jesus was kind. He helped sick people. He loved children. He forgave mistakes. He showed people what God is like. Jesus showed that God is gentle, patient, and caring.

God never pushes people away in anger. God never closes His heart. People walk away when they say no to His love, but God still waits with open arms.

Hell reminds us that our choices matter. But it also reminds us that God wants to save everyone. God never gives up easily. God's heart is always rescue. God wants to help people, not hurt them.

God's heart is always love. His love is kind, patient, and strong. God's heart is always invitation. God invites everyone to come close to Him.

That is why Christians talk about hell with kindness, not with fear. They talk about it gently because God is gentle. They want people to know that God loves them very much.

Because God's biggest wish is that no one would be lost. God wants every child, every family, and every person to feel His love.

God's story is not about punishment. God's story is about love. God's story is about forgiveness. God's story is about hope. And God's heart will always be reaching out with love.

47. Jesus Will Return

Jesus promised something very special before He went back to heaven. He promised that He would come again. He did not tell His friends the exact day or time, but He told them the reason. He said He would return to finish His beautiful rescue story.

Right now, the world still has sadness, sickness, and unfairness. People still cry. People still get hurt. Animals still suffer. Jesus knows this. He sees every tear. He hears every quiet prayer. His promise to return means He has not forgotten His world.

When Jesus comes back, He will bring peace that never breaks. He will bring justice that is gentle and true. He will bring healing to hearts, bodies, and relationships. He will gather His people and let them know they are finally home.

Jesus will not come again as a baby in a manger. He will come as a loving King. But He will not be scary. He will still be kind. He will still be gentle. He will still be full of mercy. His power will be filled with love.

Some children imagine Jesus returning with anger. But the Bible shows His heart is full of love. He comes to heal, not to hurt. He comes to gather, not to push away. He comes to finish what He started with kindness.

Jesus' return is meant to give us courage. It tells us that sadness does not last forever. It tells us that broken things will be fixed. It tells us that love will win.

When children feel afraid of the future, they can remember Jesus is coming back. When they feel small, they can remember Jesus has not forgotten them. When they feel confused, they can remember Jesus is still in charge.

Jesus returns because God never abandons His creation. He returns because God never stops loving His children. He returns because love always finishes what it begins.

The promise of Jesus returning is not about fear. It is about hope. It tells us that the story is still moving toward something wonderful.

48. God Will Make Everything New

God promises that one day He will make a new heaven and a new earth. This does not mean He will throw everything away. It means He will fix everything that was broken.

Imagine a toy that is cracked and dirty. Instead of throwing it away, someone gently cleans it, repairs it, and makes it even more beautiful than before. That is what God will do with His world.

God will heal every broken heart. He will take away every tear. He will remove fear, pain, sickness, and sadness. People will no longer hurt one another. Animals will no longer be afraid. The earth will be peaceful and safe.

The new world will be full of color, beauty, laughter, music, and joy. There will be places to explore, friends to enjoy, and love everywhere. No one will feel lonely. No one will feel unwanted.

God will not only fix the outside world. He will also heal hearts completely. People will no longer struggle with anger, jealousy, or fear. Love will fill everything.

This new world will be exactly what God wanted from the beginning. A world where people walk with Him, trust Him, and enjoy His goodness without pain.

Children often imagine heaven and the new earth as quiet or boring. But God created joy, creativity, and play. The new world will be alive with happiness and peace.

God making everything new means that no sadness is wasted. No pain is forgotten. God will turn every broken part of the story into beauty.

This promise means our hope is not just for tomorrow. It is for forever.

49. God Will Judge Fairly

God is full of love, and He is also perfectly fair. One day He will judge the world with truth, kindness, and wisdom. He will do this because He cares about everyone and wants what is good.

This judgment is not like humans judging each other. Humans often misunderstand. They only see the outside. But God sees every heart. He understands every reason, every fear, every pain, and every choice. He knows when someone is trying their best, even when they make mistakes.

God's judgment is not cruel. It is careful. He does not rush. He does not forget kindness. He does not ignore suffering. He sees everything clearly, like a bright light that shows the whole picture.

God will judge what is right and what is wrong, but He will do it with mercy and truth together. He will never be unfair. He will never be mean. He will never make a mistake. God always chooses what is loving and good.

Because Jesus carried our sin, God's children do not need to fear judgment. Jesus has already paid the price for our forgiveness. God sees us through Jesus' love. When God looks at us, He sees hope, not only our errors.

God's judgment means goodness matters. Kindness matters. Love matters. Forgiveness matters. Every small good action is important. A gentle word, a shared smile, and a helping hand are never forgotten by God. He remembers every act of love.

God's justice also means evil will not last forever. Lies will not win. Cruelty will not win. Love will win. Light will always be stronger than darkness.

God's judgment is not something to fear if we trust Him. It is something that makes the world right again. It is like cleaning a messy room so it can be beautiful and peaceful.

God wants everyone to learn, grow, and choose love. He is patient with us. He teaches us to forgive, to be brave, and to care for others. When we follow His ways, we help make the world kinder.

So we can live with hope. We can choose good every day. And we can remember that God's fair judgment is guided by perfect love.

50. Living Forever With God

Living forever with God is the most beautiful promise in the Bible. It means God's children will never be separated from Him again.

They will walk with Him like friends. They will talk with Him freely. They will feel safe, known, and loved all the time. There will be no more goodbyes, no more fear, and no more endings.

Living forever with God means waking up every day in peace. It means resting without worry. It means loving without pain. It means joy without loss.

This forever life is not boring. It is full of relationship. God will still be our Father. Jesus will still be our Savior. We will still be ourselves, but healed, whole, and joyful. We will remember our story and see how God's love carried us all the way through. We will understand how every tear mattered. We will see how every prayer was heard.

Living forever with God means finally being home. It means never wondering if we are loved. It ends in love.

For children, this promise feels like a warm hug that never ends. It is like running in a bright field without getting tired. It is like laughing without fear. It is like holding Jesus' hand and knowing He will never let go.

In that place, there will be no sickness, no sadness, and no loneliness. Everyone will help each other. Everyone will care. Animals will be gentle. Colors will be brighter. Songs will be sweeter.

Children will be able to ask God questions, and He will answer with kindness. They will be able to share their dreams and feel truly heard. They will know they are important, because God loves every heart, even the smallest one.

There will be time to play, time to rest, and time to celebrate. There will be stories to tell and smiles to share. Every moment will feel safe and good.

Living forever with God means happiness that never runs out. It means knowing we will never be alone. It means living in a light that never fades.

It is a promise of peace, joy, and endless love.
It is the most beautiful promise of all.

51. A World Made New

God promises that He will make everything new[14] . Not just a few things — everything. Every broken place will be healed. Every unfair story will be made right. Every tear will be gently wiped away.

In God's new world, there will be no more pain, no sickness, and no fear. Children will play without worrying. Grown-ups will smile without sadness. Animals will live peacefully together. No one will hurt anyone.

People will speak kindly to one another. They will help each other with joyful hearts. Being good will feel natural, like breathing. Love will not struggle to survive anymore — it will be everywhere, like warm sunlight.

This new world will still be real. It will not be a dream. We will see brighter colors, hear sweeter music, and feel deep happiness in our hearts. We will laugh together, run freely, sing loudly, and hug the people we love.

Nothing will hurt us. Nothing will scare us. Nothing will make us feel alone. God will always be close to us, like a loving Father holding His children's hands.

God is not throwing the world away. He is not forgetting it. He is fixing it. He is healing it. He is renewing it with love, patience, and kindness.

Every mountain, every river, every tree, and every flower will be full of life. The sky will be clear. The air will feel light and fresh. Everything will tell a story of peace.

In God's new world, no one will be left out. Everyone will matter. Everyone will be loved. Each person will have a special place.

The future God is preparing is not an escape from life. It is life the way it was always meant to be. A life without fear. A life without unfairness. A life full of hope.

We will wake up each day with joy. We will feel safe. We will feel thankful. We will remember that God keeps His promises.

And we will know that love is stronger than sadness, stronger than darkness, and stronger than anything else.

This is the world God is preparing: a new world, a good world, a bright world.
A world where love will never end.

---

[14] New means God will fix everything and make it beautiful and happy again.

52. Love That Never Ends

God's love will never run out. It will never fade. It will never change its mind about us. God loves us always, when we are confused, sad, happy, or tired. His love is like a light that never turns off.

In forever life, we will not wonder if God still loves us. We will not fear losing Him. We will not doubt our place in His heart. We will live inside His love every moment, like inside a warm and safe hug.

We will love God freely and with joy. We will love other people with kindness and respect. Love will no longer be fragile or temporary. It will be strong, gentle, and eternal. No one will need to hide. No one will feel alone.

Every relationship will be healed. Every mistake will be forgiven. Every misunderstanding will be gone. Every heart will be at peace. Hard words will no longer hurt, because everyone will know how to listen with love. Smiles will be honest, and hugs will be full of trust.

God's story was not made only with rules or judgment. It was not made only to teach us what is right and what is wrong. It was made to show us how much He loves us. And His story does not end with time.

It ends with love that lasts forever. And that love is waiting for us.

This love is like a sea without an end, where we can play, rest, and feel safe. It is like a home with doors always open, where no one is sent away. It is like a gentle voice that says, "You are important. You are precious. You are loved."

When we make mistakes, God does not stop loving us. When we are afraid, God stays close. When we are happy, God is happy with us. When we are sad, God comforts us. His love does not depend on what we do, but on who we are: His children.

In that world full of love, no one will cry because of loneliness. No one will be left out. No one will be forgotten. Everyone will have a special place. Everyone will know they are seen, heard, and loved.

Children will run without fear. Adults will smile without heavy hearts. Older people will rest in peace. Friends will understand each other better. Families will be united. People will be kind to one another.
There will be no more cruel words. There will be no more wars. There will be no more broken hearts. There will only be peace, joy, and love.

And we will learn to love the way God loves: with patience, with gentleness, with truth. We will learn to forgive. We will learn to say thank you. We will learn to take care of each other.

Every day will be full of light. Every moment will be precious. Every breath will be a gift.

CONCLUSION

The book ends with a message of deep hope: God's love never ends, and God's story with us never ends.

From the first lessons to the last, the book shows that God is not distant or cold. He is loving, kind, patient, and always close to His children. He created the world with love, He rescued it through Jesus, He walks with us through His Spirit, and He promises to keep us forever.

The final chapters remind us that this world, though beautiful, is still broken. There is pain, sadness, sickness, and unfairness. But God has not forgotten His world. He is not throwing it away — He is healing it. One day, God will make everything new. Every tear will be wiped away. Every broken heart will be healed. Every story will be made right.

Systematic theology for kids

In God's new world, people will live without fear. Children will play freely. Families will be united. Friends will understand one another. Love will feel natural and strong. No one will feel alone, unwanted, or forgotten.

The book also teaches that living forever with God is not boring or empty. It is full of relationship, joy, creativity, laughter, peace, and love. We will still be ourselves, but healed and whole. We will finally feel completely at home.

The very last lesson, Love That Never Ends, explains that God's love will never run out. It will never fade. It will never change its mind about us. God loves us when we are strong and when we are weak, when we are happy and when we are afraid. His love does not depend on what we do, but on who we are — His children.

Systematic theology for kids

The book reminds children that:

- They are never accidents.
- They are never forgotten.
- They are never alone.
- They are deeply loved forever.

God's story is not mainly about rules, punishment, or fear. It is about love, rescue, forgiveness, and belonging. It is about a God who walks with His children from the beginning of life into forever.

The final truth of the book is simple and beautiful:

Our story does not end in darkness. It ends in love.

And that love is waiting for us in God's heart — now and forever.

Made in the USA
Thornton, CO
04/28/26 23:14:37

078da51e-ff6f-4677-be77-8cf2f6fe341cR01